Easy

Moderate

Moderate contd.

Moderate  contd.

Tough

LEVANT & CROWN ENGINE HOUSES AT BOTALLACK

Levant and Botallack are two of the most evocative names in the history of Cornish mining. Following work by the National Trust and the Trevithick Society (named after the Cornishman Richard Trevithick who invented a steam locomotive some 12 years before George Stephenson), Levant houses the oldest beam engine in Cornwall and is once again powered by steam. The Crowns Engine Houses at Botallack are perhaps the most photographed mine remains in Cornwall, the sheer majesty of their coastal location a testament to the Cornish quest for tin and copper.

This walk allows both Levant and Botallack to be visited, the surrounding landscape littered with the remains of mine workings over the last few centuries. For this reason and as with all mining landscapes, great care should be taken to keep to the paths when walking in this area.

Refreshments & Toilets

None are encountered within the course of the walk.

Directions to start

The National Trust Levant Steam Engine House is signed from the B3306 St. Ives to St. Just road in the village of Trewellard. Park on the left shortly before the Levant entrance barrier.

Walk Directions

Leave the parking area at the far left side as you look towards the sea. A broad gravel track leads to a further parking area. From here, follow the coastal path past mine building remains as you proceed towards Botallack Head - The Brisons can be seen ahead. It is now a case of following the coastal path south as it meanders through a landscape heavily scarred by man's mining activity. The often slippery outward path passes above sheer cliffs and can be dangerous when wet or foggy.

Continue until you are on a broad track in front of the large metal mining headgear. Shortly before this, turn right and descend to visit the famous Crowns Engine Houses (it may not be advisable to descend to the lower engine house as it is not easily accessible). Afterwards, retrace your steps back to the main track, turning right to continue on the broad track ahead.

The track leaves the coastal path behind to pass in front of a large property (National Trust), this is the old Count House of the mine. The unmade track leads onto a metalled road adjacent to Botallack Manor Farm before reaching a T-junction at which you should turn left. This leads you through the village of Botallack to reach a further T-junction, again turn left. Follow the main road for about 30 yards before turning left up a lane (Cresswell Terrace) between granite cottages.

Cross the stone stile ahead and proceed across the field keeping to the left hand boundary. Cross a further stile and field in line with the telegraph poles to another stile. This time cross the field diagonally to the top right hand corner which is close to a large building now used as an Outdoor Education Centre. Over stone steps next to a wooden gate then turn immediately sharp left (almost doubling back on yourself) down a lane in front of a row of cottages. An unmade track bears to the right, passing

over a stone stile next to a metal gate. After approx. 20 yards ignore an entrance to the field on your right, bear slightly left, keeping to the boundary hedge and ignoring a further gap in the boundary hedge. Continue until you reach a stile on your right. Cross this stile and head across the field to a stile in the far left corner between farm buildings.

Turn immediately left and then right through a large wooden gate to follow the hedge boundary on your right. Reach another stone stile in the hedge on the right. Cross this stile and follow the stone boundary on your right to the corner of the field where there is a wooden stile just before another stone stile.

Cross these stiles and turn left to follow a track between hedges which descends to bear right in front of two metal gates. At a road junction, turn left to follow the road back to Levant and your car.

Easy

WALK NO.

1

DISTANCE

3 MILES

TIME

2 HRS

MAP REF.

ORDNANCE SURVEY
LANDRANGER 203

368
345

MÊN-AN-TOL, NINE MAIDENS & THE DING DONG MINE

The Penwith Peninsula in the far west of Cornwall has long been recognised as a site of international importance in the understanding of ancient man's early activities. Stone circles, standing stones, burial chambers and hill fortifications are all found in the area in significant numbers, many dating back to 2,000 years before the birth of Christ.

This walk, with extensive views across treeless open moor and pastoral farm land, passes the famous Mên-an-Tol stones before reaching Men Scryfa, a weathered inscribed stone commemorating Rialobran who is believed to have been a sixth century chieftain. The Nine Maidens stone circle is also encountered before reaching the Ding Dong Mine engine house. The mine is a distinctive feature on the skyline and though closed for over 70 years, remains an impressive monument to Cornwall's once widespread tin mining industry.

Refreshments & Toilets

Lanyon Farm Tea Rooms - seasonal opening hours or booking for parties out of season.

Directions to start

From the B3306 St. Just to St. Ives road, turn south, just east of Morvah signed towards Penzance and Madron. A small roadside parking area is reached after approximately 1 mile. (If travelling from Penzance, take the Madron road passing Lanyon Quoit on your right).

Walk Directions

From the parking area, follow the farm track that leads off opposite the granite building of the Mên-an-Tol studio, constructed in 1882. It is about 10-15 minutes walk through a quiet almost lonely landscape to the Mên-an-Tol stones, the distinctive profile of a mine engine house to your right is that of Ding Dong Mine which will be encountered later. Mên-an-Tol is reached via a path through gorse after crossing stone steps on your right (signed).

After visiting Mên-an-Tol, retrace your steps back to the farm track. Turn right to head north once again, a stone stile next to a gate on your left is the entrance to a field containing the inscribed standing stone of Men Scryfa. Return to the main track, this time turning left to assume the northward route. Continue ahead until reaching a track fork in front of the remains of a granite building. Here, bear right onto a grassy track passing the remains of the granite building (left) before reaching a metal gate.

From this point follow an obvious path ahead across moorland towards the rise in the land ahead (the Ding Dong Mine is distant right). The path climbs before bearing right to reach the nine remaining stones of the Nine Maidens stone circle (an overgrown set of smaller stones is passed on the way and should not be confused with the much grander Nine Maidens that are your target). A well worn path leads from the stone circle to the Ding Dong Mine engine house, St. Michael's Mount can usually be seen in the distance as the views

open up across Mount's Bay.

Standing with your back to the chimney at the front of the engine house, turn right to follow a track across a stone stile next to a gate gap. The rough track heads towards the distant farm buildings of Lanyon Farm. Pass over a small stone stile next to a metal gate and follow the track through scrubland before reaching a metal gate and continuing between stone walls. On reaching the road, turn right and proceed past Lanyon Farm back to the parking area.

Easy

WALK NO.

2

DISTANCE

3 MILES

TIME

2 HRS

MAP REF.

ORDNANCE SURVEY
LANDRANGER 203

418
345

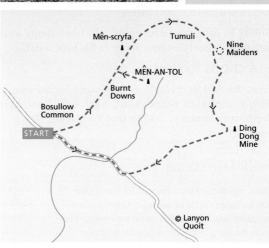

ST IVES, CARRICK DU & CLODGY POINT

The historic fishing centre of St. Ives is a popular destination for visitors to west Cornwall, the narrow streets, busy harbour and golden beaches providing a draw throughout the year. St. Ives is of course famous for the artists who have been drawn here since the late nineteenth century by the area's clear light, mild climate and stunning landscapes.

This walk quickly leaves behind the everyday bustle of the town to follow the coastal path from which small fishing boats can usually be seen. A further highlight is the vista across Porthmeor Beach to the award winning building of the Tate St. Ives, now one of Cornwall's major attractions. The return inland is via clearly marked fields and stiles which provide views across St. Ives Bay towards Godrevy Lighthouse.

Refreshments & Toilets

Toilets in car park (start point). Refreshments available at Porthmeor Beach. All other facilities a short distance away in St. Ives itself.

Directions to start

From the A30 near Hayle, follow signs for the coach park in St. Ives. Pass coach park and leisure centre to roundabout, bear left, then right into Carnellis Road, sign posted Porthmeor, continue and follow Porthmeor Beach sign, down a steep hill. Car park is on your left.

Walk Directions

Walk up the steps adjacent to the toilet block, turning right along a tarmac lane running just above the putting green. The path bears right after a bowling green towards the small rocky headland of Carrick Du (from where there are lovely views back across the sands of Porthmeor Beach to the Tate St. Ives building).

10

A broad coastal path (signed Zennor) leads off towards Clodgy Point. Pass through a kissing gate and following a yellow arrowed waymark post. Several paths proceed ahead to a large inlet which has developed through coastal erosion and land slippage. Follow the coastal path around this crevice using stepping stones in the muddier areas. The path provides enjoyable sea views before reaching a large rock just to the left of the path you are following.

Here, turn left to follow a path inland that climbs towards a stone wall. Thrift, foxgloves and pink campion cover this landscape in summer. Follow the track to a path T-junction where a National Trust sign indicates the start of the property known as Hellesveor Cliff. Turn left in front of a stone wall, keeping it to your right as you climb away from the coast. The rural track proceeds through a farm gate before reaching a stone stile on your left just as the track bears around to the left (opposite two farm gates). Climb the stile noting the first of a series of black and white posts that will act as a guide back to St. Ives.

Follow the grassy path across stiles keeping to the left hand edge of the fields. The black and white posts point to the view across St. Ives Bay towards Godrevy Lighthouse. After crossing the last in a series of east facing stiles with black and white posts, turn left down the edge of the field to cross a stile and follow a narrow lane. Cross the stile at the bottom of the lane, turning right onto a lane which runs through a secluded residential

area. At a T-junction, turn left and follow the road as it winds its way down into St. Ives. This eventually turns sharp left to proceed downhill back to the car park.

Easy

WALK NO.

3

DISTANCE

3 MILES

TIME

2 HRS

MAP REF.

ORDNANCE SURVEY
LANDRANGER 203

515
408

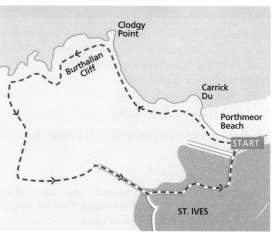

11

GODREVY LIGHTHOUSE & NAVAX POINT

Godrevy Head provides the northern boundary of St. Ives Bay, the adjacent broad expanse of Gwithian Towans proving a magnet for surfers and families alike. The highlight of this walk is the close proximity to Godrevy Lighthouse, built in 1859 and inspiration for Virginia Woolf's 'To the Lighthouse'. The coastal path continues around Navax Point and above Smugglers and Fishing Coves before returning to Godrevy where there is a modern cafe.

Refreshments & Toilets

Modern cafe at start point. Toilets available adjacent to National Trust parking area at Godrevy Head.

Directions to start

From the B3301 Hayle to Portreath road, turn off signed to Godrevy adjacent to a narrow bridge close to the Sandsifter Hotel. Park in front of the cafe building. (If full, a further N. T. parking area is available further on nearer the lighthouse).

Walk Directions

From the parking area in front of the cafe, head back onto the metalled road and turn left, following the coastline towards the lighthouse (if low tide, an alternative is to walk along the beach before rejoining the coastal path). St. Ives can be seen just across the bay. As you enter the National Trust property of Godrevy, keep to the lower coastal path as this provides the closest views across to the lighthouse.

As the path rounds the headland, a climb onto a broader track reveals Navax Point ahead. Follow the broad grassy path, eventually leading through a kissing gate to climb through gorse and on to reveal the many coves on this part of the north coast. Following the coastline, the path through the gorse leads to stone steps into a field.

Keeping to the left boundary of the field, pass over a stone and wooden stile, following a broad track off to the left. The track turns inland to reach a parking area on the main road. (NB - As the remainder of this walk is now by road without a path, walkers with children etc. might prefer to turn around and return by the outward route).

Turn right onto the main road, proceeding back downhill to the parking area at Godrevy.

Easy

WALK NO.

4

DISTANCE

3.5 MILES

TIME

2 HRS

MAP REF.

ORDNANCE SURVEY
LANDRANGER 203

585
423

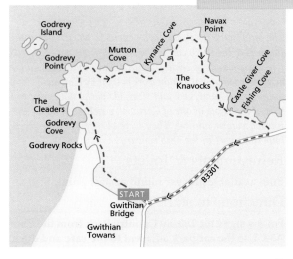

13

RESKAJEAGE DOWNS & TEHIDY WOODS

The local name for Reskajeage Downs is North Cliffs, in many ways a more accurate description of this part of the north coast. The open clifftops encountered at Reskajeage Downs are in sharp contrast to the woodlands of Tehidy Country Park that make up the second half of this circular walk. The 250 acres of woodland at Tehidy were bought by Cornwall County Council in 1983, resulting in over nine miles of woodland, lake and riverside paths now open to the public. The woodlands were originally part of the estate of one of Cornwall's richest families, the Bassetts, whose fortune was derived from tin and copper mining. They were also responsible for the development of nearby Portreath as an important port in the 18th century.

Refreshments & Toilets

Both available all year round at start point.

Directions to start

Follow signs for Tehidy Country Park from the Camborne junction (signed A3047) on the A30. Use the car park adjacent to the cafe and duck pond.

Walk Directions

Return to the car park entrance and turn left, following a tarmac road marked to Tehidy Park. The road proceeds ahead, between houses and a golf course to reach a kissing gate at the top (footpath sign). Walk on and pass through a gate at the top into Tehidy Park Woods to reach a path junction. Bear left signed to "Lake via Otter Bridge". A broad track leads ahead, passing housing on the left before reaching Kennels Hill crossroads.

Turn right (signed to North Cliffs car park), climbing slightly uphill. At a T junction at the top, bear right. At a further path junction, keep right again. At the next T junction (waymark post with coloured arrows), turn left and walk straight ahead to emerge from the woods into North Cliffs car park. Continue to the main road and then turn right to walk along a grassy bank. After a short distance, cross the road to take the first left down a rough track to reach the National Trust parking area at Basset's Cove.

Leave the parking area left to follow the coastal path above the cliffs. Offshore are Crane Islands and views towards Godrevy Island and lighthouse. The obvious path proceeds between fields and gorse, passing through three kissing gates on the way. At a small parking area overlooking the sea, bear left to the main road and cross to a stone stile on the opposite side. Descend alongside the hedge, passing through a kissing gate and continue in the next field. A track between bushes leads to a gate and a road.

Turn left and adjacent to a cottage at the end of the road bend, turn left to take a central track which leads into Tehidy Woods. Now follow the broad tree lined track (West Drive) ahead for over 1 mile. Where the path divides shortly after a mini waterfall, keep to the right hand path straight ahead, eventually reaching a T junction.

Turn right, crossing the stream and then bearing immediate left (signed to the Lake). Walk ahead, to the right of the stream and where the path forks, keep to the left. Keep ahead at a bridge and walk alongside a series of stepped mini waterfalls. Now follow the obvious path alongside the lake, using a boardwalk and on to round the head of the lake. Bear right at a path junction (with two bridges in sight of each other), crossing the footbridge to reach a further duckpond. Now walk the short distance back to your car.

Easy

WALK NO.

5

DISTANCE

4 MILES

TIME

2 HRS

MAP REF.

ORDNANCE SURVEY
LANDRANGER 203

649
434

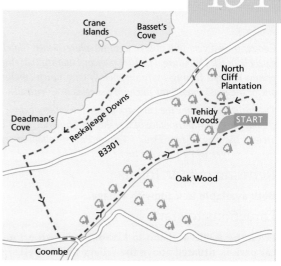

15

CADGWITH & THE DEVIL'S FRYING PAN

Cadgwith is a gem of a village with its whitewashed thatched cottages clinging to the hillside above a pebble beach providing a picture postcard quality that draws visitors throughout the year. The cove retains a small fishing tradition though on a much smaller scale than when it could boast of being one of the most important pilchard fisheries in Cornwall.

The walk starts from the car park above the village before passing the attractive Grade Church, the second most southerly place of worship in England. After reaching the coastal path, the route passes around the magnificent Devil's Frying Pan, a collapsed sea cave with a narrow arch through which the sea surges when tides are high.

Refreshments & Toilets

Both available in Cadgwith village.

Directions to start

From the A3083 Helston to Lizard road, turn off and follow signs to Cadgwith. A large car park is situated above the village and is well signed.

Walk Directions

Return to the entrance of the car park and turn right to walk up the metalled road. On reaching a road junction shortly after a pair of granite pillars, turn left and continue ahead past a further road leading off to the left. After a hundred yards, next to parallel telegraph poles, take a path left, away from the road as indicated by a public footpath sign. Pass left over a stone stepping stile to arrive in a field.

Head across the field aiming for the telegraph pole to the left of the church tower as you look towards it. This leads to a small stone stile in the hedge. After the stile, proceed towards the church keeping to the right hand boundary of the field. A stile provides access to the churchyard. After exploring the churchyard at your leisure, leave via a stile next to the small double gates at the far side of the church. A track leads left to a gate before reaching a road.

Turn left and follow the quiet country lane which provides occasional glimpses of the sea. Continue past the first public footpath sign on your right to follow the road around to the left as it passes a farm. The white dishes of the Goonhilly Earth Satellite Tracking Station can be seen across the fields to the left.

After the farm, the lane runs parallel with the coast before reaching a sharp left bend. Here turn right and cross a stile next to a farm gate indicated as a public path (signed Studio Gulval). Follow the track in the direction of the sea. In front of a gate that leads to a bungalow, take the right hand path that leads to the coast path. Views in the distance are of a white castellated building (Lloyds Signal Station - now owned by the National Trust) and the lifeboat station.

At the bottom of the path, bear left in front of a stone stile and continue on the coastal path north towards Cadgwith. In time, this passes around the impressive Devil's Frying Pan with its 200 foot drop. Emerge into a clearing keeping straight ahead to pass a house and through a gate to a road. Turn right down a metalled lane, passing "Ruan", a National Trust house. After a bench, the path leads through pretty gardens at around "Hillside" to cross a stone stile. Walk ahead, descending slightly to reach a T junction. Turn right to visit the village and cove (note on your way down in front of a thatched cottage the sign indicating the footpath back to the car park). This path leads past the corrugated church of St. Mary's and through a pleasant valley.

WALK NO.

6

DISTANCE

2.5 MILES

TIME
IN HOURS

1.5 HRS

MAP REF.

ORDNANCE SURVEY
LANDRANGER 203

719
149

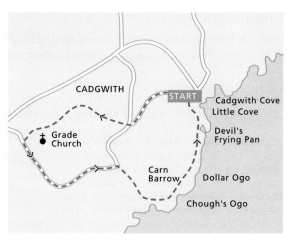

17

GILLAN CREEK & ST. ANTHONY-IN-MENEAGE

Helford village on the glorious Helford River is the starting point for this five mile circular walk. Peaceful woodland paths and open countryside are traversed before reaching Manaccan Church. The famous fig tree growing from the medieval church walls is believed to be centuries old and is said to bring bad luck to those who pick the fruit. Gillan Creek provides a delightful approach to the waterside Norman church at St. Anthony-in-Meneage. Turning west, the final part of the circuit follows the coastal path alongside the Helford River, on a shady woodland path that passes several tiny coves.

Please Note:

Part of this walk uses a concessionary footpath from which dogs are banned.

Refreshments & Toilets

Toilets in Helford car park (start point). Pubs at Manaccan and Helford village. Cafe and general stores and post office are in Helford village.

Directions to start

From the B3293 Helston to St. Keverne road, follow the signs for Helford via Newtown-in-St.Martin. Park in the car park above Helford village, overlooking the river estuary.

Walk Directions

Turn right out of the car park following the road down into Helford village. If refreshments required, cross footbridge into village, otherwise continue ahead and bear left up a lane adjacent to the road bridge, signed as a public footpath to Manaccan. After a short distance, the lane continues as a public footpath past a large thatched cottage into a lovely area of woodland.

As the stream becomes more apparent, the path forks. Keep straight ahead eventually crossing the stream via a stone bridge and onto a stone stile. Continue on the woodland path, crossing 3 further stiles to enter a field.

Cross the field diagonally on a traceable

path to the corner of a hedge. From here, bear right (public footpath sign) and climb to a metal gate and stile. At the road turn left for 20 yards before crossing a stile on the right. Cross the field, keeping left, over a stone stile to run alongside a garden fence. Pass into the cul-de-sac before turning right down the main road and into Manaccan Church grounds. The fig tree can clearly be seen growing from the wall. Pass the church to leave by a gate and follow the road ahead to the left of the vicarage. After a short distance turn right signed to Carne.

Descend to cross a stile, entering a field and keeping to the right. Cross a further two stiles in the field corners before continuing through a lovely wooded valley crossing stiles and a bridge over a stream. At the road, turn left and shortly afterwards follow the road left signed to St. Anthony alongside Gillan Creek to reach the waterside church. Pass in front of the church and bear around to the left to pass the churchyard gate. Immediately afterwards bear right and then turn right to follow a concessionary path through the Bosahan estate (NB no dogs allowed).

Pass through a metal kissing gate and after approximately 40 yards, turn left up the side of the field. Just short of the top of the field in the corner, continue through a metal kissing gate to arrive on the coastal path alongside the Helford River. Skirt the field to pass a gateway where there are two sea-marks.

Pass over two further stiles before taking a right turn shortly after entering a field. Pass through a metal kissing gate and follow the narrow, often shady woodland path.

The path emerges adjacent to a small cove, bear left for a few yards before following the yellow waymark arrow right to continue once again on the woodland path. A kissing gate leads to a second cove with a boathouse and onto a third cove before eventually emerging in front of some buildings. Assume the metalled lane before turning right at the road. Shortly after the 'Old Pilchard Shed', turn left up some steps signed to the coastal path. A wooded lane leads to two metal kissing gates and an entrance into Helford car park, on the right of the second gate.

Easy

WALK NO.

7

DISTANCE

5 MILES

TIME

3 HRS

MAP REF.

ORDNANCE SURVEY LANDRANGER 204

759
261

Helford River

Bosahan Cove

Helford

Treath

The Gew

START

St. Anthony-in-Meneage

Gillan Creek

Manaccan

HELFORD & FRENCHMAN'S CREEK

The pretty village of Helford is set within the lush, tranquil surroundings of the Helford River, a paradise for wildlife and favourite spot for boating enthusiasts. From the quiet wooded valley at Helford, this walk crosses fertile farmland before descending to run alongside the National Trust owned Frenchman's Creek, made famous by Daphne Du Maurier's novel of the same name. This is one of Cornwall's special places and you will often see herons here during the course of your walk. Completion is via the picturesque Penarvon Cove before returning to Helford once again.

Refreshments & Toilets

Toilets within Helford car park (start point). Refreshments in Helford at the pub, cafe or general stores and post office.

Directions to start

From the B3293 Helston to St. Keverne road, follow the signs for Helford via Newtown-in-St. Martin. Park in the car park above Helford village, overlooking the river estuary.

Walk Directions

Turn right out of the car park following the road down into Helford village. If refreshments required, cross the footbridge into village, otherwise continue ahead and bear left up a lane adjacent to the road bridge, signed as a public footpath to Manaccan. After a short distance, the lane continues as a public footpath past a large thatched cottage into a lovely area of woodland. As the stream becomes more apparent, the path forks right to cross the stream and passes over a small stone stile. Head up through the woodland and pass over a further stile to ascend a field, keeping to the right hand side. Walk through a gate at the top of the field, and continue to the left of the farmhouse at Kestle and through a gate opening to reach the road.

Cross the road to the opposite footpath and down the right hand side of the field before turning right through a gate. Descend via a broad woodland track to reach a National Trust sign indicating a permissive path along Frenchman's Creek leading off to the right. Follow the path alongside the creek, crossing three small footbridges in the process.

Shortly after crossing the last footbridge, the path forks next to a large tree on the left. Take the right hand path, climbing some steps. A steady climb is rewarded with magnificent views across the Helford River. On reaching a kissing gate, turn right up the lane. At the brow of the hill, turn around for one last view over the Helford River before turning right along a track signed to

Helford via Penarvon Cove.

Cross a cattle grid and turn left (signed to Pengwedhen and Helford). Descend, keeping right at a path fork alongside a telegraph pole numbered DP30 to reach the tiny cove and beach. Cross the beach, bearing right to leave the beach and take the path on your immediate left to continue the walk which then climbs away from the cove. The path bears right alongside a wall and through a metal kissing gate. Turn left down a lane in front of a white house, bearing around to the right at the bottom to pass the pub and walk through Helford village. Cross the footbridge and return back up the hill to the car park.

Easy

WALK NO.

8

DISTANCE

3 MILES

TIME

2 HRS

MAP REF.

ORDNANCE SURVEY
LANDRANGER 204

759
261

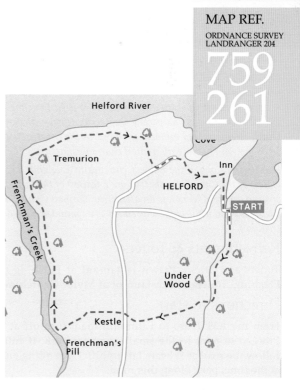

21

FLUSHING & MYLOR CHURCHTOWN

The attractive village of Flushing, from where this walk starts, has a history indelibly linked with neighbouring Falmouth. The deep natural harbour of the Carrick Roads river estuary led to the development of Falmouth as an important port; from the end of the seventeenth century Falmouth was at the centre of the packet ship service that transferred mail around the British Empire. The Dutch engineers and builders involved in the construction of Falmouth Harbour helped establish a settlement at Flushing, its genteel charm making it popular as a home for retired packet ship captains.

Flushing has one of the mildest climates in England, largely due to its proximity to the sheltered waters of the Carrick Roads that are a feature of this walk. Half way around the walk at the popular boating centre of Mylor, is an attractive Norman Church with an ancient 17' high Celtic Cross. The graveyard and walls of the church act as a reminder of the dangers associated with the area's maritime tradition.

Refreshments & Toilets

Toilets and Sticky Prawn restaurant at Flushing Quay, Post Office and two pubs in Flushing. Toilets and restaurant at Mylor Churchtown.

Directions to start

From the A39 Truro to Falmouth road, turn off at Penryn to follow signs to Flushing. Proceed to park in the small quay car park. If full, turn right out of the car park and follow the road as it bears left uphill. Depending on the parking restrictions in operation at the time, park along this road.

22

Walk Directions

After parking the car, (beside the road in this instance), walk forward towards a metal gate at the end of the road indicating Trefusis Estate. Continue on, ignoring the path to the right, passing around adjacent to a heavy stone wall and through a small area of woodland that leads to a granite grid next to a metal gate. From here, the route follows an open path around Trefusis Point, through fields and gorseland, crossing a stream, stiles and gates en route. The Carrick Roads river estuary is on your right all the way to Mylor Churchtown.

Just before Mylor, cross a stile next to an old concrete bunker, after a further stile take the path which runs along the water's edge in front of Restronguet Sailing Club. At Mylor you will find a sizeable marina, public toilets and a restaurant. Follow the road along the water's edge, passing the toilets on your left. Bear round to the left, up the hill to reach the church lychgate and take a few minutes to explore the ancient church and see the Celtic Cross.

Leave the churchyard via the lychgate and take the public footpath directly opposite. This leads to a metalled road that follows the course of Mylor Creek for about three quarters of a mile. At the road junction, turn left and continue the walk up this road until you reach the top of the hill and onto where another road crosses in front of you (this is the Flushing to

Mylor road).

Directly opposite, you will see two granite posts marked "Trefusis Estate Private. Public Footpath Only". Take this route. In a few yards you will cross a cattle grid, immediately after which, turn right over a stile indicating the public footpath to Flushing. Follow the hedge to a stone stile facing you. Over the stile and turn right immediately. Proceed downhill beside the hedge until you reach houses at the bottom of the field. In the right hand corner of this field, over a stile and down a short lane. Down steps, turn right and drop down into the village. Bear left at the Methodist Church and return either to your car if parked on the quay car park, or walk past the car park to the end of the village, sharp left up the hill and back to your car.

Easy

WALK NO.

9

DISTANCE

4.5 MILES

TIME

2.5 HRS

MAP REF.

ORDNANCE SURVEY
LANDRANGER 204

807
338

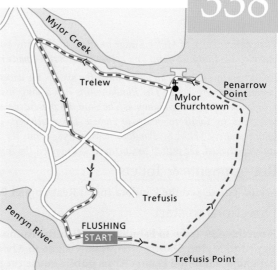

MYLOR BRIDGE & RESTRONGUET CREEK

The genteel charm of Mylor Bridge provides the starting point for a largely creekside route that offers views to Restronguet Point and across the Carrick Roads river estuary to the Roseland Peninsula.

Conveniently situated half way around the walk is the waterside Pandora Inn, one of Cornwall's most famous watering holes. The Pandora Inn has a long history and was originally a 13th century farmhouse before being known as The Ship. Its present name is as a result of a Captain Edwards who was sent to Tahiti to bring to justice the mutineers against Captain Bligh on The Bounty. Unfortunately, H.M.S. Pandora was wrecked on its return journey and Captain Edwards courtmartialled. He retired to Cornwall and named the inn after his last command.

Refreshments & Toilets

Mylor Bridge and the Pandora Inn at Restronguet Passage.

Directions to start

From the A39 Truro to Falmouth road on the Falmouth side of Perranarworthal, turn off signed to Mylor. Shortly after, follow signs to Mylor Bridge. Park in the free small car park adjacent to the Lemon Arms public house car park.

Walk Directions

Turn left out of the car park and proceed up the main street past the Lemon Arms pub. After a short distance, turn left opposite a newsagent onto the main Truro road. Opposite the school, turn right into Bells Hill. Follow the quiet country lane for approximately half a mile to the top of Bells Hill where you will bear left.

Shortly afterwards, passing the Tregunwith Farm Caravan and Camping Club entrance, turn right down a track signed with public footpath sign. Where the path looks to divide into three at Halywn, keep right (i.e. third path) and follow the track downhill noting the now excellent views across the creek.

The route ahead crosses two cattle grids, eventually descending to Tregunwith Woods creekside. Pass a large white house into an area of light woodland keeping the creek to your left before eventually arriving at the famous Pandora Inn.

Walking in front and away from the inn, still keeping the creek on your left, bear to the right at a private garage, following a track between the signs marking "Littlewood" and "Dolphin Cottage". The path descends to a beach, where at high tide a private path can be used by the public, before bearing left at Restronguet Weir following a public footpath sign to Greatwood. Keep to the path just above the creek before reaching a clearing by some houses and bear right up a hill following a public footpath sign to Mylor Bridge.

The castle like appearance of Greatwood House appears before you, from where you continue up the hill for about 100 yards before turning left to follow the public footpath sign to Mylor Bridge. Pass through a series of metal gates and kissing gates following mainly the creekside path around the peninsula back towards Mylor Bridge. Once an area of housing is approached, bear left following a green public footpath sign attached to a private garage wall and continue past the Post Office into the village and your car.

Easy

WALK NO.

10

DISTANCE

4.5 MILES

TIME

2.5 HRS

MAP REF.

ORDNANCE SURVEY
LANDRANGER 204

803
362

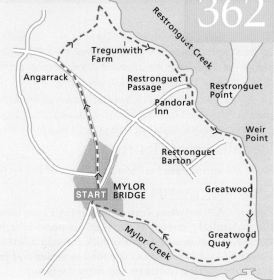

25

CIRCULAR WALK AROUND COOMBE CREEK

A popular walk with locals given its brevity and the excellent views afforded across the River Fal and the tidal creek at Coombe. The deep waters of the Fal estuary are an ideal location in which to lay up unrequired ships- there are usually a couple of cargo carriers here to provide a stark visual contrast to the otherwise sedate woodland landscape.

Though the start of this walk is by road, it is largely traffic free and not long before you are on woodland paths to the creekside hamlet of Coombe. The area is well known for its Kea Plums, a visit in late summer or autumn will invariably find local produce on sale at cottage gates.

Refreshments & Toilets

None are encountered within the course of the walk.

Directions to start

From the A39 between Truro and Playing Place, turn off left to follow signs for Porth Kea (be particularly careful as the turn off point is rather acute from the main road). Leave Porth Kea and proceed up the hill, passing a left hand turn for Old Kea. Park close to Lower Lanner Farm where the road is wider and fringed with trees (please take care to avoid obstructing traffic to and from the farm).

Walk Directions

Continue along the road, travelling in the same direction as when you arrived, ignoring footpaths and the road signed to Coombe. Pass a pair of cottages on the left hand side and follow the road as it meanders a little before climbing towards Higher Trelease Farm. As the road turns left (farm entrance straight ahead), notice the views to the right across fields towards Truro Cathedral.

Follow the road round to the left which eventually descends to reach a junction, the right hand route having a public footpath sign to Coombe. For the moment, take the left hand fork to follow a farm track down to a metal gate. Go straight on through the gate and follow the narrow path down to a small riverside beach area. This provides views across the River Fal to the thatched Smugglers Cottage restaurant. *(This diversion is not a Public Right of Way but is generally open to allow responsible walkers to enjoy the view).*

Turn back from the river and retrace your steps to the road junction. Now follow the footpath indicated to Coombe through a gateway. (Dog owners - lead needed due to horses). As you approach the renovated farmhouse, turn right up a track to a gate with a wooden stile. Continue along the left side of the field and straight on over three more stiles (views of the river to the left again). The third stile leads off to the left onto a woodland path.

Later, there are views to the left

across Cowlands Creek to the wooded Roundwood Point with its ancient quay. The tunnel like effect of the route ahead is caused by a mixture of old plum trees and overgrown hedges. Descend to reach a lane, turning right to walk to the creek-side hamlet of Coombe.

Round the inlet and take the public footpath to Lower Lanner Farm that is signed between two houses. Climb between gardens on a concrete and grass track. When the track turns left to Cowlands, continue straight on up a narrow track to reach a stile. Climb the field diagonally up to the top right hand corner and a wooden gate. From the gate, climb to a group of trees on the horizon. At the trees, turn right to a gate and continue down the left side of the field. As you descend, note the views to the right. At the bottom, a metal gate leads back onto the road and your car.

Easy

WALK NO.

11

DISTANCE

2MILES

TIME

1.5HRS

MAP REF.

ORDNANCE SURVEY
LANDRANGER 204

837
414

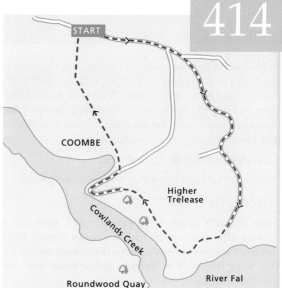

START

COOMBE

Higher
Trelease

Cowlands Creek

Roundwood Quay

River Fal

PORTHMELLIN HEAD & THE PERCUIL RIVER

In the space of only 3.5 miles, this walk allows the visitor to enjoy the classic elements that make the Roseland Peninsula some of the finest walking country in Cornwall. From the National Trust Porth Farm, a route passes above Towan Beach with views across the sea to Nare Head and Dodman Point. After crossing the peninsula via the hamlet of Bohortha, the return journey is a woodland walk alongside the delightful Percuil River, home to boat moorings and wildlife alike. A medieval tide mill dam can be seen at Froe Basin, shortly before the end of the walk.

Refreshments & Toilets

Toilets at National Trust Porth Farm (start point).

Directions to start

From the A39 Truro to St Austell road, take the A3078 signed to St Mawes. Turn off shortly after the hamlet of Trewithian signed to Gerrans. Pass through Gerrans. After approx 2 miles you reach the parking area on the right. (Alternatively, reach Gerrans via the King Harry Car Ferry signed from the A39 at Playing Place between Truro and Falmouth).

Walk Directions

From the car park at Porth Farm, cross the road and pass through the farm building housing the toilets. Head right towards the beach, taking a further right on to the coastal path just before the beach. Pass the coastguard practice post to walk through a gate and follow the coastline around Killigerran Head and Porthmellin Head, crossing a stile enroute. The path eventually rounds Porthbeor Beach, a sheltered cove favoured by locals and visitors alike. On reaching the main access down to the beach, turn right, heading across the field to a stile next to a N. T. sign.

Turn right onto the road before taking the first left to Bohortha. Pass through the hamlet and follow the unmade lane ahead (past a postbox) indicating a public footpath to Place Quay. The track passes two gates on the right before reaching a path junction at the bottom of a track between two hedges. Turn right over a stile before bearing left downhill with views across to Place House and St Anthony church spire. Pass through a kissing gate and past a row of six trees to follow a track adjacent to a wire fence and through a kissing gate.

Do not pass over the stile onto the road, instead maintain a path at the bottom of the field signed as a public footpath to Porth Farm (1.5 miles). It is now a straight forward ramble through the attractive woodland alongside the Percuil River, known as Drawler's Plantation (N.T.).

Eventually the track bears around

to the right into Porth Creek. Continue ahead ignoring a right detour to Bohortha, over a stile into a field. At the end of the field cross over another stile and continue ahead on the path. Ignore a further right detour to Bohortha, eventually entering a field to pass in front of Froe basin. The path crosses the stream via a wooden footbridge, after which turn right along a grassy path that returns to Porth Farm and your car

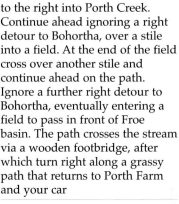

Easy

WALK NO.

12

DISTANCE

3.5MILES

TIME

2HRS

MAP REF.

ORDNANCE SURVEY
LANDRANGER 203

868
328

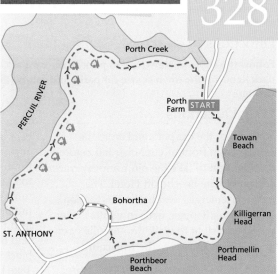

29

NEWQUAY TOWN WALK & PENTIRE POINT EAST

This might seem something of an unusual choice for a walk given the large percentage of the route that is undertaken through the built up area of Newquay. There is however, much of interest for the walker and this walk provides an excellent introduction to a busy resort that is uniquely different to any other in Cornwall. Newquay's growth as a centre for tourism was assured by proximity to fine beaches; the arrival of the railway in the late nineteenth century led to the large Victorian hotels that can be seen today.

The walk leads away from Newquay's busy harbour to the well preserved Huer's Hut; from here the Huer would direct fishermen to encircle the great pilchard shoals that once visited the bay. Towan Head leads to the famous Fistral Beach before continuing to Pentire Point East where there are superb views across the sand dunes at Crantock and the River Gannel Estuary.

Refreshments & Toilets

Throughout the course of the walk though toilets in particular can be closed in low season.

Directions to start

Follow the signs in Newquay to park in the car park adjacent to the railway station. If full, park in one of the town centre car parks and follow directions from either the bus station or harbour.

Walk Directions

Walk out of the car park and cross the main road in front of you. Bear left before turning right to take the old tramway track adjacent to the Beechcroft Hotel. The tramway emerges next to the Bus Station (toilets usually open, even in winter), after which turn right to walk through the open grassed area known as the Killacourt.

Shortly before steps to the Sealife Centre,

bear left and walk to descend via steps adjacent to the Cliffside Hotel. Bear left through a small parking area, cross the road and take a right hand path up through an open space where there are public seats overlooking the beach. Steps lead to a metalled lane alongside the West End Bowling Club before passing a toilet block and turning right into Fore Street. Take the first right into South Quay Hill to visit the harbour.

From the harbour either A) if the tide is low: cross the harbour sand to climb steps in front of the Harbour Hotel, reaching the metalled lane at the top or B) if the tide is full: retrace your route back up South Quay Hill, turning right and then first right at the Red Lion Pub to walk down North Quay Hill to reach the Harbour Hotel.

Follow the metalled lane from the Harbour Hotel towards the sea. Where the lane forks, bear left (the right fork leads to the harbour again) and climb steps adjacent to a white house. A gravel track leads up to the Huer's Hut where there is an information plaque and wide ranging views across Newquay Bay.

Take the coastal path that follows the cliff in the direction of Towan Head (the view right is across Watergate Bay to Trevose Head with its lighthouse). Off to the left is a large, granite war memorial as well as the imposing red brick Headland Hotel. Follow a path to the old lifeboat station where there is an information plaque before taking the opportunity to make the short climb to the lookout shelter on Towan Head.

Return from the headland past the old lifeboat station before turning right to walk in front of the Headland Hotel. Cross over Fistral Beach or via the path that runs to the rear of the sand dunes next to the golf course. At the end of Fistral Beach, climb steps and turn right along a road in front of hotels. The road eventually becomes an unmade track and

passes in front of bungalows before bearing left and gaining height to reach East Pentire car park. Here, take the opportunity of walking out onto the headland and enjoy the views across Crantock Beach and the River Gannel.

After walking on the headland, return to the car park and proceed ahead up the main road through the built up area of East Pentire. The sheer number of hotels testify to the holiday accommodation needs of one of Britain's biggest resorts. Continue for about one mile before reaching the junction of Esplanade Road.

Cross and take the path running up the side of the Golf Links, bearing left at the top where there is a parking area. Continue into the residential area of Atlantic Road, crossing the main road into Crantock Street and walking downhill to cross the road into Newquay's town centre. Continue until you reach the bus station once again. Rejoin the tramway and walk back to your car next to the railway station.

Easy

WALK NO.

13

DISTANCE

4MILES

TIME

2.5HRS

MAP REF.

ORDNANCE SURVEY
LANDRANGER 200

812
617

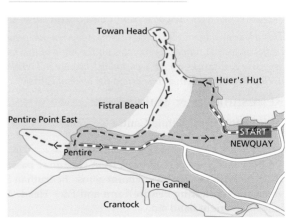

31

PARK HEAD & THE BEDRUTHAN STEPS

Though the two coastal properties indicated in the title of this walk are adjacent, few will have heard of the former whilst images of the latter have adorned Cornish souvenirs for over a 100 years.

Owned by the National Trust since 1966, the 200 acre property of Park Head is rarely busy; even in the high season you will often only have the cries of seabirds for company. It is far removed from the bustle of Newquay, just a few miles down the coastline. It was the growth here of Victorian tourism that inevitably led to the popularity of the Bedruthan Steps. The name derives from the legend that the rock stacks were used by a giant called Bedruthan as steps to achieve a short cut across the bay.

This whole area was well known to Iron Age Man, his presence indicated by the existence of two cliff castles as well as numerous barrows on the route of this walk. Though only the rough outline of the defensive earthworks can be seen today, they are nonetheless thrilling reminders of man's activities in the area dating from a time before the birth of Christ.

Refreshments & Toilets

Bedruthan Steps Visitors Centre (seasonal).

Directions to start

Take the B3276 north coast road from Newquay passing through Mawgan Porth. One mile after the National Trust viewpoint across Bedruthan Steps at Carnewas, turn left at a small green sign indicating Pentire Farm and Park Head. A small parking area is located up the lane on the right hand side.

Walk Directions

Walk up the lane, for the time being ignoring the footpath left which leads to Pentire Steps and Park Head. Shortly before Pentire Farm, follow the coastal path sign right across a step stile next to a farm gate. At the end of the garden wall, bear diagonally left across the field to pass over a further stile adjacent to a gate. Continue in the same direction towards the valley, passing through a kissing gate in the bottom corner of the field. Follow the valley path to the sea at Porth Mear, in the wetter areas the route uses boardwalks to provide safe passage.

Follow the coastal path to the left of the cove, passing the National Trust sign for Park Head and a wooden kissing gate. The path bears left around a series of coves and where the cliffside has weakened. After passing a short piece of stone wall, the path forks. Keep right and head towards a small stone memorial in commemoration of the person who donated the property to the National Trust. From the memorial, bear right out to the promontory of Park Head. Where the promontory narrows, notice the ditch and rampart that once formed part of the defensive fortification of an Iron Age cliff castle.

Return to the memorial and bear right following the coastal path. You will soon reach a kissing gate indicating a path back to the car park. Ignore this and walk to a further kissing gate and around the sandy cove of Pentire Steps.

Where the path splits after a section of wall, take either as they soon rejoin continuing to obtain excellent close-up views of Bedruthan Steps. Climb adjacent to a wire fence and pass around above the steps. Where the boundary wall on your left bends off to the left, notice undulations on the coastline to your right. These are the earthworks constructed thousands of years ago to protect the Redcliff Castle.

As much of the remainder of this walk now has to be by road, you may want to turn around here and retrace your route back to the Pentire Steps kissing gate passed earlier which will return you to your car.

At a waymark post which indicates the coastal path, proceed ahead to the visitor centre. Turn left and follow the road back to the entrance to Park Head and Pentire Farm, returning to your car.

Easy

WALK NO.

14

DISTANCE

3 MILES

TIME

2 HRS

MAP REF.

ORDNANCE SURVEY
LANDRANGER 200

854
707

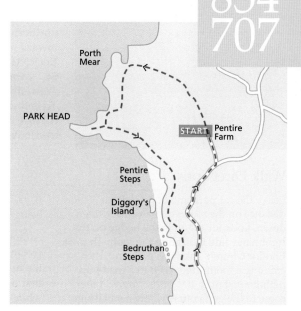

DAYMER BAY & ST ENODOC CHURCH

A chance to visit the small, Norman church of St. Enodoc with its famous crooked spire is one of the highlights of this enjoyable walk. The church's location, among drifting sand dunes that border the Camel estuary, has ensured a constant battle with nature to prevent the building being lost forever. Its present condition seems a far cry from when a nineteenth century vicar had to enter the building by skylight to hold a service!

The graveyard provides the final resting place for Sir John Betjeman, the Poet Laureate who spent a great deal of his childhood in the area and eventually had a home in the nearby village of Trebetherick. The dazzling light and estuary views that were such an inspiration to him make this a popular ramble that can be enjoyed throughout the year.

Refreshments & Toilets

At Daymer Bay car park in season (start point). Further refreshments often available at Rock with toilets at the Rock Quarry car park (half way).

Directions to start

From the roundabout on the A39 at the northern end of Wadebridge bypass, turn toward town centre, take signs to Pityme and Rock. After reaching the Pityme Freehouse at St. Minver Lowlands, turn right into Trewiston Lane and follow signs for Trebetherick. From here, turn left to follow a narrow lane signed to Daymer Bay. Park overlooking the beach.

Walk Directions

Leave the car park and backtrack for a short distance on the road you have just driven down. Look for a sign in the hedge on the right hand side indicating the footpath to St. Enodoc Church. Take this path and after crossing a footbridge, keep to a made-up path for just over 100 yards. You will then come to the golf course where a small sign warns you of the possibility of golf balls being hit from the right.

Although you can see the made-up path recommence again across the fairway in the direction of the church, do not head in that direction but bear left and follow the white footpath stones up towards the gate.

This route will still take you to the church but in a clockwise direction. It is important to follow these instructions closely because there are many other paths across the golf course, some for the exclusive use of players.

You will shortly come to dual yellow arrows on a post. Turn right here towards the church, still following the white stones and note the views to your right across the Camel estuary to Stepper Point. The small tower on the headland was used by mariners as a navigational aid. On reaching the church, the grave of Sir John Betjeman can be found on the right, shortly after the lychgate. After leaving the church, turn right and follow the stones in an anti-clockwise direction positioned around the green below the church.

Bear left around the back of the green and follow the marking stones up the valley which runs beside a stream on your right. Keep following the stones and turn right over a footbridge constructed beside a pond. Bear left after the pond, up a track and turn left on to a metalled road at a waymark post. Almost immediately you will see a slightly larger white stone on your right. DO NOT turn right here but walk past the stone into a small parking area. At the rear of the parking area, another path, with a white stone positioned at the top, rises slightly on your right. Follow this path and the white stones through the middle of the course, eventually you will see the clubhouse in the distance. Cross a gravel track, the route

bears right to pass the St. Enodoc Golf Club sign, before turning left to run beside a wire fence.

Continue ahead with the fence on your immediate right. Once you have reached a stone encased bench, the track bears right to descend to an unmade road. Turn left and then right so that you walk down the hill to Rock.

At the bottom of the hill turn right and walk along the side of the estuary (Padstow is situated opposite). Continue to the end of the road, entering the Rock Quarry car park where there is a toilet block. Turn left out of the car park to follow the coast path signs. Depending on the state of the tide, the return journey to your car can either be along the beach to Daymer Bay, or through the sand dunes and around Brea Hill on a well marked coast path that runs parallel to the estuary.

Easy

WALK NO.
15

DISTANCE
3 MILES

TIME
2 HRS

MAP REF.
ORDNANCE SURVEY
LANDRANGER 200
929
777

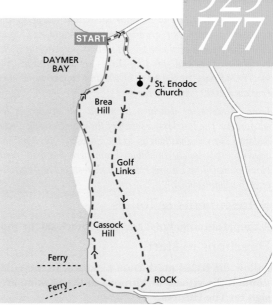

35

THE HURLERS & THE CHEESEWRING

The bleak wilderness of Bodmin Moor is a world apart from the traditional images of a Cornish landscape. A land of granite tors and windswept open moor, this walk explores a landscape containing some of the most important evidence of prehistoric man in the country. Stone circles, burial chambers and standing stones are all found in large numbers here as well as signs of a more modern activity in the form of tin and copper mine engine houses, once part of an industry that employed 4000 people in the area.

From Minions, at nearly a thousand feet above sea level Cornwall's highest village, this walk encounters The Hurlers, a series of three large stone circles built over 4000 years ago. Next target is Rillaton Barrow and then on to the Cheesewring, a naturally occurring granite rock formation that appears precariously unstable. From here the walk continues along a track before reaching the Housemans Mine Engine House, now restored and containing excellent displays on the history of the area (free admission).

Refreshments & Toilets

A shop, tea-room, hotel and toilet block can be found in Minions village.

Directions to start

Follow the B3254 north from Liskeard. In the village of Upton Cross, turn left and pass through the village of Minions to the parking area on the western side indicated by a sign for The Hurlers.

Walk Directions

Leave the car park at the top left hand corner via steps next to an Information Board describing the stone circles. Head across a grassy plain to visit the Hurlers stone circles. These circles are in alignment with the Rillaton Barrow in the north and when you proceed along this imaginary line, the Barrow can be seen quite clearly as a grassy rise in the hillside before you. This is the site of a burial chamber in which a gold cup, now in the possession of the British Museum, was found. From this point it is only about 1/4 mile distance from the Cheesewring.

Heading in the direction of the Cheesewring a number of paths lead through tumbled granite rocks to a tremendous vantage point across the surrounding countryside. It is here that you will find the Cheesewring itself, an unusual granite rock formation situated on the edge of the quarry. Note also the granite rocks of nearby Stowes Hill that have been weathered into unusual formations.

Walk down from the Cheesewring on the easiest route i.e. with the quarry behind you, keeping the Caradon Hill television transmitter to your left. You will very shortly come to a grassy path by a long ditch. Walk beside this ditch for about 200 yards keeping it to your left until you reach a fenced area of old mine workings. At this point you hit the track (once the route of the tramway that was used to transport quarried granite).

Continue on the track for about twenty minutes and shortly before a house ringed by trees,

bear right to visit the restored Houseman's Mine Engine House. This contains a fascinating insight into prehistoric and modern man's activities in the area and has free admission as part of the Minions Area Heritage Project.

From the engine house, return back towards the tree ringed house and resume your original direction to reach the road that leads through Minions village. Turn right to return to your car.

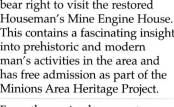

Easy

WALK NO.
16

DISTANCE
2.5 MILES

TIME
1.5 HRS

MAP REF.
ORDNANCE SURVEY
LANDRANGER 201

259
712

Cheesewring

Quarry

DITCH

Fenced mine workings

Rillaton Barrow

TRACK

THE HURLERS

Engine House

Car Park

Car Park (Western Side) START MINIONS

37

SIBLYBACK, GOLITHA FALLS & KING DONIERT'S STONES

If you absolutely hate road walking of any sort, even the relatively quiet moorland roads that you will find on this route, then this is not the walk for you (similarly, walkers with very small children might find it wiser to pick an alternative walk, just in case). The reason for its inclusion is that it allows a visit to the three elements of the walk's title in a reasonably short circular route. Siblyback Lake is one of South West Water's main Cornish reservoirs and a popular watersports centre and recreation area. Golitha Falls is a series of small rapids where the River Fowey passes through a lush, wooded granite gorge; a particularly attractive area affording plenty of opportunities to enjoy a packed lunch. Lastly, King Doniert's Stones mark the believed burial site of a Cornish King who drowned in the River Fowey in the ninth century. All of this, combined with an inland moorland setting, make the route a welcome alternative to the more traditional Cornish coastal walk.

Refreshments & Toilets

At Siblyback Lake (S.W. Water). Toilets also at Golitha Falls parking area.

Directions to start

Siblyback Lake is signed (brown tourist signs) from the A38 at Dobwalls. Park overlooking the lake and dam or in a free parking area just before the entrance to Siblyback.

Walk Directions

Walk back out of the recreation area, crossing a cattle grid and turning right past the alternative parking area. Ignore a public footpath on the left of the road and walk on to reach a path on the right, through a gate, signed to the dam. Follow the path around the edge of the reservoir to pass through a kissing gate adjacent to the dam.

Keep straight ahead, over a cattle grid, descending on a metalled lane. At the bottom, bear left and walk across a further cattle grid and down to a large metal gate that marks the entrance to the South West Water property.

At the road, turn left. The road climbs before descending to pass cottages and reach a road on the right. Turn right and join a path on the left through woodland alongside the River Fowey to Golitha Falls. After visiting the falls, retrace your steps back to the road and turn right across the river bridge and then right again to continue up to a T junction. Here, turn left and walk up the road to reach King Doniert's Stones. After the stones, return to the main road and continue in the direction you were originally travelling. The Caradon television transmitter can be seen ahead of you.

Walk down to take the left turn signed to Siblyback Water Park. Proceed ahead, over a stream and following the road past houses, climb a little to reach South Trekeive Farm which is on your right. On the far left side, after the tractor shed, take the public footpath (marked with a green footprint sign) and walk up to a metal gate. Continue up a farm track between hedges and pass into a field at the top.

Cross straight ahead towards a gate. Shortly before reaching the gate, cross to the other side of a small stone wall and pass through an adjoining gate. Cross the field ahead towards the dam. Pass through a gate and turn right, returning to your car via the route around the reservoir used earlier.

Easy

WALK NO.
17

DISTANCE
3.5 MILES

TIME
2.5 HRS

MAP REF.
ORDNANCE SURVEY
LANDRANGER 201
238
707

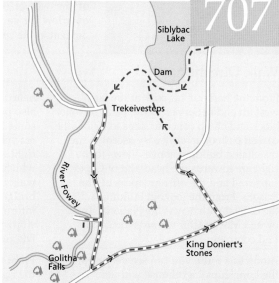

39

SENNEN COVE, LAND'S END & NANJIZAL BAY

The surfers' paradise of Sennen Cove is the starting point for this thrilling walk around the far western tip of England. Though Land's End itself is fairly developed, the weathered granite landscape and views towards the Longships Lighthouse and Isles of Scilly make this route a must for the walker in Cornwall. The route continues around the beautiful turquoise waters of Nanjizal Bay before heading inland to Sennen, home of many 'first and lasts'. Views on the return to Sennen Cove are across the stunning Whitesand Bay towards the headland of Cape Cornwall and the offshore rocks of The Brisons.

As with all walks with a western facing coastline, this route is particularly enjoyable in the late afternoon when a setting sun provides a magnificent backdrop to the rock and seascapes.

Refreshments & Toilets

Sennen Cove (start point) The Old Success Inn, Sennen Land's End complex. Refreshments available in Sennen.

Directions to start

Follow the A30 towards Land's End, turning off for Sennen Cove. Park in one of the car parks at either end of the village (toilets at both). In high season, an overflow car park is available on the right before the descent to the cove.

Walk Directions

From the harbour car park at the far western end of Sennen Cove, pass the toilet block and climb concrete steps to follow the coastal path on a fairly easy ascent to the castellated building above. Views to the right are towards the headland of Cape Cornwall and the offshore rocks of The Brisons. From the lookout building, follow the coastal path across the National Trust owned Mayon Cliff towards the Land's End complex.

Along this route you can see very clearly the Longships Lighthouse with its

helicopter landing pad. On a clear day, it is also possible to make out the Isles of Scilly, some 28 miles away. Shortly before reaching the Land's End complex, fork right to pass the First and Last House which houses a small gift shop. From here, walk over the spectacular suspension bridge above a deep chasm, a small information sign details the chasm's shipwreck history. An interesting Wildlife Discovery Centre is to the right.

From the Land's End Hotel, drop down to the right, over a wooden bridge and head for a white house called Greeb Cottage. On the footbridge is a sign detailing the local history of the area. Turn right shortly before the Greeb Cottage complex before bearing left onto the coastal path to pass the animal petting area.

Continue ahead, through a spectacular granite landscape, off to the right is the much photographed arched rock known as Enys Dodnan. After passing through an old granite boulder boundary, the views ahead are across Mill or Nanjizal Bay. Above the blue green waters of the bay is a large white house, continue in this direction.

Just before the steps which lead to the beach at Nanjizal, turn left on to a defined path which climbs up the near side of the valley (i.e. the opposite side to the house). This climb is steep but it is not long before the path levels to run parallel with a stone wall on your left. At the end of the path/wall, pass left through a large kissing gate and cross the field on the obvious path ahead. Sennen church tower can be seen off to the right. Pass through a gate following the right hand field boundary. At a gate opening, cross the next field diagonally, turning right at the hedge boundary to follow the edge of the field. Sennen church tower comes once again into view.

Continue over a stone stile next to a gate, passing a farm to reach a T-junction. Cross the lane to take a stone stile in front of you which leads through a concreted farmyard. Cross the farmyard to pass over stone steps ahead,

beside a gate. Follow the right edge of the field past a granite cross in the adjacent field heading towards the cottage in front of you. At the end of the field, cross a stone stile and pass through a gate and over steps to walk across the driveway of the cottages. Although this is a public right of way, as always, take care to avoid disturbing the occupants.

Cross the road and continue straight ahead to join the main road, turning right towards Sennen. Pass the First and Last Inn and Sennen church on the main road.

Just before a petrol filling station, turn left on to a footpath adjacent to a white cottage. Follow the footpath over stiles, take the right fork, cross lane before descending to reach Sennen Cove once again.

Moderate

WALK NO.
18

DISTANCE
5.5 MILES

TIME
3 HRS

MAP REF.
ORDNANCE SURVEY
LANDRANGER 203
349
264

The Tribbens

START

Pedn-men-du

Sennen Cove

A30

Mayon Cliff

Dr. Syntax's Head

Sennen

LAND'S END

Dr. Johnson's Head

B3315

Enys Dodnan

Trevescan

Trevilley

Pordenack Point

Trevilley Cliff

Nanjizal

TREEN, PORTHCURNO & PORTH CHAPEL

The area covered by this walk is one of the most stunningly scenic areas in west Cornwall. From the delightful small fishing cove of Penberth where brightly coloured boats wait patiently on the slipway, the coastal path climbs to pass Treryn Dinas, the site of an Iron Age hill fort, before reaching the famous headland of Logan Rock. The 60 ton rocking stone which gave the headland its name has sadly lost much of the sensitivity of balance for which it was famous, having been dislodged in 1824 by a young naval officer. A compensation however, is the incredible view across turquoise seas to the white sands of Porthcurno Beach, one of Cornwall's best, before climbing to the unique Minack Theatre, literally carved out of the cliffside.

Refreshments & Toilets

Toilets, shop and pub at Treen (start point). Toilets and refreshments at Porthcurno.

Directions to start

Follow signs towards Lands End on the A30 from Penzance. After the village of Drift, proceed onto village of Catchall before taking B3283 signed to St. Buryan. A little over a mile after St. Buryan, turn left into the hamlet of Treen and drive past the pub to park in a large car park at the end of the hamlet.

Walk Directions

Walk back through the hamlet past the pub to reach the main road once again. Turn right before quickly taking a further right signed to Penberth. Follow the tarmac road to the pretty fishing cove below. Cross the stream in front of the sea by turning right across the slipway in front of the capstan restored by the National Trust. This was the original method of hauling boats from the sea before the modern day winch which is now used.

Ascend the coastal path adjacent to the wooden winch house. A fairly steep route zig zags up the cliff side. At the top, a well worn path through gorse crosses a flat plateau, Logan Rock is revealed to your left.

Continue on to cross a small stream via a boardwalk before eventually reaching a path junction. Turn left to visit Logan Rock, otherwise turn right. After only 10 yards, the path splits. Keep left (the right fork returns to your car at Treen) and then take a further left fork to remain on the coastal path. The views across turquoise waters to Porthcurno Beach and the Minack Theatre headland are outstanding. The path emerges at a further junction. Here, take the second path on the left indicated by a coast path sign (the first descends to the beach). Pass between two concrete bunkers before reaching a waymark post in front of a gate. Here, cross the stone stile, which is close to the National Trust Porthcurno sign and bear left to follow the coastal path in the direction of the large red and yellow cable warning sign.

Bear right towards Porthcurno Beach and as you descend, note steps leading from the beach up the opposite cliffside towards the Minack Theatre. Cross the beach to these steps and ascend the cliffside or alternatively skirt the beach and continue on the coast path marked to Porthgwarra.

Pass adjacent to the Minack Theatre before crossing the car park and walking through a wooden and stone kissing gate. The coastal path follows the bottom of field boundaries to reach a path junction at the start of the National Trust headland of Pedn-men-an-mere. Follow the coastal path which passes above the beautiful sandy cove of Porth Chapel Beach. Cross a small wooden footbridge before climbing away from Porth Chapel Beach to pass the holy well of St. Levan.

Shortly after the well at a waymark post, leave the coastal path (which continues left) to continue straight ahead on a narrow track. The track emerges to cross a metalled lane to enter the churchyard on the opposite side. Bear left to circle the church, leaving via an excellently preserved coffin stile, the path from which is waymarked.

Cross the field to climb stone steps (with a wooden gate) before continuing across a path between fields heading for the farm buildings in front of you. A stone cross is passed half way across.

Pass through a metal kissing gate next to a wooden farm gate before bearing left across a parking area to a further metal kissing gate. Turn right after the gate to follow the track along the edge of the field. The dormitory type building marked Eastern Telegraph Co that can be seen ahead was part of the Cable and Wireless operation here, now the Museum of Submarine Telegraphy (well worth a visit). Follow the track downhill through a gate to reach a road. Turn right and cross the road to pass through a gap in the wall.

Follow a tarmac drive, turning left at a waymark post and follow path uphill to pass through a gate. Follow the path as it meanders right before crossing a stone stile beside a metal gate. Head across the field towards farm buildings, passing through the gate gap in the opposite field boundary and over a second field. Continue into a third field, heading diagonally towards a telegraph pole to the right of the farm buildings and pass over a wooden stile which is adjacent to a metal gate.

Follow the track to the right of the farm, passing a metal gate on the right. As you approach the main farmhouse, cross a large stone stile on your right before turning left to follow the field boundary. At the top left hand corner of the field, cross a stone stile and over the field to a further stile and field. Cross a stile next to a wooden gate and over a further field. Cross fields via three further stiles before walking along a lane next to a house. Continue to the road before turning right to get back to your car.

Moderate

WALK NO.
19

DISTANCE
4 MILES

TIME
3 HRS

MAP REF.
ORDNANCE SURVEY
LANDRANGER 203
395
228

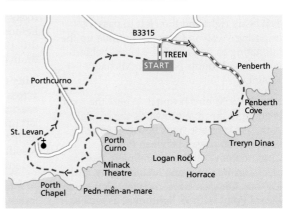

43

MOUSEHOLE & LAMORNA COVE

The picture postcard qualities of Mousehole and Lamorna Cove draw visitors and locals to this area throughout the year. The quintessential Cornish fishing harbour of Mousehole (locally pronounced Mouzel) was a favourite subject of the Newlyn School of Painting, established in the nineteenth century and drawn by the area's clear light and stunning seascapes.

The idyllic cove at Lamorna with its turquoise blue waters and granite harbour wall is revealed in all its glory on the approach from the coastal path. The weathered granite landscape through which Lamorna is reached makes the experience all the more unforgettable.

Refreshments & Toilets

Mousehole (start point) and Lamorna Cove.

Directions to start

Take the A30 to Penzance and follow signs to Newlyn. From Newlyn, follow signs to Mousehole. Roadside parking and a pay and display village car park are found on the outskirts of Mousehole.

Walk Directions

Head for Mousehole, passing the Old Coastguard Hotel. A short distance after the hotel, turn left away from the road following a metalled lane next to a high wall. After a few twists and turns, you emerge above Mousehole harbour (toilet block). Round the harbour passing the War Memorial and the Ship Inn, the latter has a memorial plaque to a previous landlord lost in the Penlee lifeboat tragedy.

Follow the road after the Lobster Pot Hotel as it bears right and then left to pass the imposing Weslyan Chapel. Continue up the hill noting as you climb the views behind you across Mounts Bay to St. Michael's Mount.

Pass the wild bird hospital. Where the road bears right, head left towards the coastal path. The unmade track between large houses soon passes between fields. Continue now on the coastal path, passing an overgrown ruin and an old coastguard lookout. On clear days, the views left are to Lizard Point with its lighthouse as well as the Earth Satellite tracking dishes of Goonhilly.

At a waymark post, the coastal path descends left down steps before passing over a brook via granite boulders. Climb some granite rock steps before passing through the Kemyel Crease nature reserve. From here onwards, the coastal path is much easier going.

Follow the coastline before rounding the rocky headland of Carn-du (views to Lamorna Cove and the lighthouse Tater-du). Proceed to Lamorna Cove through a dramatic granite landscape.

After exploring the harbour, head back across the concrete bridge to the start of the coastal path upon which you arrived. Fork left up a grassy path indicated by a public footpath sign. The path climbs through woodland and wild flowers to lead past the old granite quarries.

At a farmhouse, bear right on a footpath indicated by a yellow waymark arrow.

Follow the farm track through the farm and past a further farmhouse. As the track bears left away from the farm next to a metal gate, cross a stone stile adjacent to a waymark post and proceed over the field keeping to the left hand boundary. Cross a stone stile before heading across the field to a gate.

Cross an adjacent stone stile and head for the corner of the wall in front of the farm buildings ahead. Cross a stile with a footpath sign. Turn left along a farm track, passing between farm buildings to assume a metalled lane before bearing right across a stone stile adjacent to a metal gate and footpath sign. The path keeps to the left of the meadow to pass over a further stone stile.

Take the narrow path to a third stone stile and onto a stone bridge and stepping stones. Follow the narrow track which becomes a broader track. Cross a farm lane to a public footpath sign and then cross a stone stile and three wooden stiles between farm buildings. Pass through a small wooden gate into a field bordered by farm buildings on your right.

Cross a stone stile beside a Cornish cross. Head across a field to a stile next to a gate (a standing stone is below right). Keep to the left hand boundary. Pass over a stone stile next to a gateway into a smaller second field with a stile in the corner (a standing stone is below right in this field also). Cross the stile into a third field, again via the left edge towards a stone stile in the opposite boundary. Cross a further field

and stile into the next field, passing over a stone stile next to a metal gate.

Turn right on the road and then immediate left beside Raginnis Cottage to enter Raginnis Farm. Keep on the farm track to the right of the farmhouse (keeping a thatched cottage on your left). Cross a stone wall stile close to a metal gate. Keep to the boundary of the field before crossing left over a stile shortly after a metal gate.

Cross the field in the direction of St. Michael's Mount to a stone stile in the opposite edge. Mousehole village is now in view. Head across the next field to a further stile, also close to a metal gate. Cross the field diagonally to a gate in the hedge, pass down a few stone steps, turn left on to a track for ten yards and take a narrow path which leads off to your right. Turn right to descend via a steep lane with a stream running alongside. Proceed into Mousehole and return to your car.

Moderate

WALK NO.
20

DISTANCE
4MILES

TIME
3HRS

MAP REF.
ORDNANCE SURVEY
LANDRANGER 203
475
268

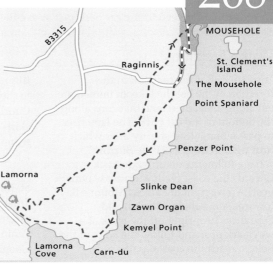

PRUSSIA COVE & CUDDEN POINT

This walk follows a glorious part of the coastline on the eastern side of Mount's Bay, the jagged rocks on the National Trust headland of Cudden Point providing a distinctive target from the start point of Perranuthnoe. After Cudden Point, tiny coves and inlets indicate you have reached the famous smuggling coastline of Prussia Cove. In the late eighteenth century, this area was the domain of the famous smuggler John Carter, whose fascination with Frederick the Great, King of Prussia, led to the naming of the area.

After Prussia Cove the route turns inland to walk back over open countryside that provides stunning views across Mount's Bay with its fairytale island castle of St. Michael's Mount.

Refreshments & Toilets

Toilets in car park (start point). Refreshments available in season above Perranuthnoe Beach. Public house in the centre of Perranuthnoe village.

Directions to start

From A394 Penzance to Helston road, turn off for Perranuthnoe (between Marazion and Rosudgeon). Proceed to the car park just above the beach.

Walk Directions

Turn left out of the car park in the direction of the beach. Take an immediate left along a metalled lane that runs along the bottom of the car park. The lane rises to pass a bungalow, shortly after which, turn right in front of "Blue Burrow" cottage following an unmade track towards the coast (yellow arrow waymark post). Views right are across Mount's Bay towards Mousehole, Newlyn and Penzance. Turn right off the track at a waymark post and follow the edge of the field to reach the coastal path.

It is now a case of following the coast path to the jagged headland in the distance, Cudden Point. The route crosses stiles and skirts fields, the large building that can be seen high above Stackhouse Cove on the left is Acton Castle. Views progressively open up over your right shoulder towards St. Michael's Mount. From the National Trust headland of Cudden Point, note the distant clear day views to the Lizard Peninsula with the satellite dishes of Goonhilly Earth Station.

From Cudden Point, keep to the coastal path passing lichen covered posts and the National Trust sign. The coastal path passes around both Piskies and Bessy's Coves. At Bessy's Cove, the path passes an old fisherman's stone cottage and wooden hut, bearing left towards houses above the cove.

In front of the gate of the thatched cottage, turn right up an unmade track to reach tall granite posts at the start of a driveway. Turn left to follow the track leading away from the coast. Walk ahead, climbing gradually to reach a line of granite posts dividing the track in two. Keep to the left hand side (the right being a private drive) and at the top of the lane turn right on to a metalled road.

Follow the road as it twists and turns for approx. half a mile to reach a hamlet with farm buildings on your right. On your left, opposite the farm buildings is a public footpath sign indicating a track (adjacent to a bungalow called "Cuddan-Rose").

Take the track and pass over a wall stile next to a metal gate and cross the field keeping to the left hand boundary. After a further wall stile in the left hand corner of the field, keep to the right hand boundary of the next field noting once again views across Mount's Bay. Pass to the right of a garage and through a wooden gate to cross a lane. Where the unmade lane turns left towards a disused farm building, keep ahead (right) on to a track marked with a public footpath sign.

Turn right into a field indicated by the same sign post opposite, following the meadow edge left up to a stone stile in the top of the field. On entering the next field, cross right keeping to the right. Once again there are superb views across Mount's Bay and St. Michael's Mount.

Head towards Trebarvah Farm, crossing a stile adjacent to a metal gate. Pass through the farmyard left, heading for an open gateway with disused stile to the right and with a public footpath sign next to a barn. Pass across the right hand side of a meadow heading towards Perranuthnoe village. Cross a stile and two fields before following a narrow track to a stone step stile with a metal bar. Cross a further field in line with the telegraph poles, through a metal kissing gate and onto a tarmac lane. Turn left at the main road, passing through the village to return to your car.

Moderate

WALK NO.

21

DISTANCE

4MILES

TIME

2.5HRS

MAP REF.

ORDNANCE SURVEY
LANDRANGER 203

540
295

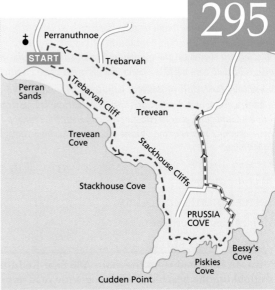

Perranuthnoe

START

Trebarvah

Perran
Sands

Trebarvah Cliff

Trevean

Trevean
Cove

Stackhouse Cliffs

Stackhouse Cove

PRUSSIA
COVE

Bessy's
Cove

Piskies
Cove

Cudden Point

47

PORTREATH & RAPLH'S CUPBOARD

It is hard to imagine modern day Portreath as the busy, industrial harbour that existed in the 18th and 19th centuries. Huge amounts of copper ore were brought from the inland mining areas by railway and stored on the quayside. Steam ships took the ore to South Wales for smelting, returning with coal that was used to power the Cornish mine engines.

Nowadays Portreath provides a popular surfing and family beach as well as the starting point for a coastal walk above dramatic cliffs. The National Trust owned Western Hill leads to the awesome Ralph's Cupboard, a deep chasm created when the roof of a large sea cave collapsed. Legend has it that this was home to a fearsome giant who ate fishermen though sea birds and grey seals are a more likely sight today!

The latter part of the walk necessitates some road walking and this should be considered if your party has young children.

Refreshments & Toilets

All facilities in Portreath.

Directions to start

Portreath is signed from the main A30 near Redruth via the B3300. Park in the car park overlooking the beach or beside the wide road approaching the beach car park.

Walk Directions

Returning to the main road, turn right on the bend to proceed between houses up Battery Hill, Portreath Beach is below you to your right. The seabird colony of Gull Rock soon comes into view. The lane descends near the far end of the beach before bearing right and in front of two garages turning left with a sign indicating the north coast footpath. A track climbs gradually uphill to reach a National Trust sign indicating Western Hill.

Here, take the right hand path. Climb the headland keeping the sea in view to your right which will soon bring you above high cliffs with Gull Rock closer in view. Follow the coastal path through the gorse, the odd detour from the main path can be taken to maintain the sea views.

The path rounds a section of the heavily eroded cliff and provides the first views over the deep fissure that is known as Ralph's Cupboard. Stay right, on the coastal path. Continue around above Ralph's Cupboard taking particular care near the edge of the steep cliffs.

As the coastal path continues (via a kissing gate), Godrevy Island and Lighthouse can usually be seen in the far distance. The path descends to a waymark post indicating Carvannell Downs. Follow the steep path down into the valley before climbing out on the opposite side. Continue above Porth-cadjack Cove with Samphire Island just off shore.

Descend via granite steps to cross a small boardwalk over the tiny stream that runs down to the sea.

After the boardwalk, climb steeply on a path that runs adjacent to a wire fence (ignore a right bearing seaward path that leads from the boardwalk also). Walk alongside the wire fence. At a stile, turn left and follow the path right to reach a parking area (Bassett's Cove).

From here, turn left away from the sea and walk up to the road. Turn left and follow the road back towards Portreath for approx. 1.5 miles. As the road bears left overlooking the village, take a small path next to a stone bench on the right hand side of the road. This path zig zags down the hill, at the bottom turn left to return to the car park.

Moderate

walk no.

22

distance

4 MILES

time

2 HRS

map ref.

ORDNANCE SURVEY
LANDRANGER 203

655
454

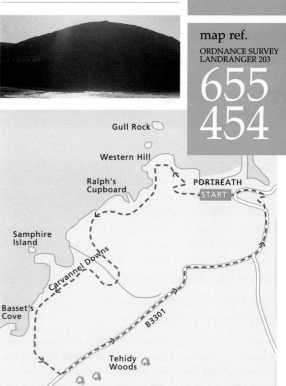

49

MULLION COVE & PREDANNACK HEAD

The harbour at Mullion Cove is a common view on Cornish postcards and books, its sturdy granite walls dating from the end of the 19th century when there was still a lifeboat station here as well as a thriving fishing industry. The harbour and the winch house at the head of the slipway have been in the care of the National Trust since the end of the Second World War.

From the car park, the walk crosses farmland to pass an ancient stone cross. On reaching the coast path, the walk returns to Mullion Cove around Predannack Head, the route providing far reaching seaward views to St. Michael's Mount and just offshore, to Mullion Island.

Refreshments & Toilets

Both available in Mullion Cove.

Directions to start

From the A3083 Helston to Lizard road, turn off opposite the Mullion Holiday Park signed to Mullion Cove. After Mullion village itself, the road leads to one of two car parks serving Mullion Cove. The first is the larger and on the left. The second is Porthmellin car park and is found on the right, a short distance further on. Park in either.

Walk Directions

From either car park, follow the tarmac road towards the cove. Shortly after leaving the car park turn left at a public footpath sign adjacent to a telegraph pole and ascend the gravel track to the right of the Criggan Mill holiday site. Continue up the hill past the first right turn to Polpeor to reach a further public footpath sign on the right.

Cross the stone stile and field, keeping to the left hand boundary to reach a stone step-stile. Four further step-stiles are encountered before entering a field containing an old stone cross in the far left corner. After the cross, pass over a further step-stile and traverse the field via the left hand boundary. A track leads over a stile in front of a cottage to emerge onto a metalled lane. Turn left to follow the country lane to a T-junction. Turn right and follow the lane towards the sea.

Cross a cattle grid next to the National Trust sign indicating Predannack Wollas. At a National Trust parking area, bear left through farm buildings to pass over a wooden stile next to a large gate. A track next to a lane crosses a tiny stream and wooden stile before climbing for a short distance to a National Trust sign indicating a right turn to the cliff. Follow the sign and after crossing a stile, take the right fork. Within a short distance turn right which puts you on a direct course for Predannack Head and Mullion Cove.

Encountered on the way is a stile, a gate next to an English Nature sign and a further gate. Goonhilly Earth Satellite Tracking Station can be seen to the north, on a clear day St. Michael's Mount can be seen in the far west.

The coastal path drops to a small stream in a narrow valley in front of a large white house before climbing to a wooden stile. Continue on the coastal path before descending to the harbour. After visiting the cove, turn right to follow the road uphill back to the car parks.

Moderate

WALK NO.

23

DISTANCE

4.5 MILES

TIME

2.5 HRS

MAP REF.

ORDNANCE SURVEY
LANDRANGER 203

672
180

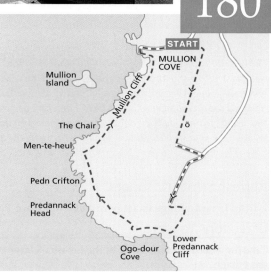

START
MULLION COVE

Mullion Island

Mullion Cliff

The Chair

Men-te-heul

Pedn Crifton

Predannack Head

Ogo-dour Cove

Lower Predannack Cliff

LIZARD, HOUSEL BAY & BASS POINT

The Lizard Peninsula is not surprisingly familiar to walkers with Lizard village at the very tip of the peninsula offering a myriad of routes popular for escorting the visitor around England's most southerly point. After passing the old lifeboat station and lighthouse, this walk allows a visit to the collapsed sea cave known as Lion's Den. From here you round the beautiful Housel Bay with its clear blue waters to the Lloyds Signal Station now owned by the National Trust. From Bass Point the route leads to the new lifeboat station before turning inland past beautiful thatched cottages at Church Cove. The historic church at St. Wynwallow, England's most southerly place of worship, provides a rewarding end to a walk packed with plenty to see.

Refreshments & Toilets

Within Lizard village (start point) and at Lizard Point.

Directions to start

Take the A3083 from Helston to the Lizard. A large free car park is available in the centre of the village.

Walk Directions

From the telephone boxes in the centre of the village, head to the left of the Top House public house and follow the road which becomes indicated as Penmenner Road. The top of the Lizard Lighthouse can be seen across fields off to the left.

The road leads onto an unmade track signed as a public footpath. Descend on the obvious track to the right of a large house, eventually becoming a narrow track as it descends towards the sea. On reaching the coast path, turn left across a footbridge, climbing steps to soon pass above the old lifeboat station. Pass the cafe and buildings at England's most southerly point as well as the interesting record of lives saved by the lifeboat station. Assume the coastal path towards the lighthouse.

Just after the lighthouse take a right hand diversion towards the sea, passing with great care to the Lion's Den, a collapsed sea cave. (Note that the Lion's Den is situated on the side of the point looking across Housel Bay).

Return to the main coastal path, descending via steps to cross a footbridge at Housel Bay. After climbing steps on the opposite side, turn right at an acorn waymark sign to pass adjacent to the Housel Bay Hotel. Continue on the walk, head towards the castellated building of Lloyds Signal Station and follow the coastal path below the station and onto Bass Point with its coastguard lookout and red daymark wall.

Shortly after the cottages adjacent

to the coastguard lookout, the coastal path bears right and continues to the new lifeboat station before descending to the tiny inlet of Church Cove. Turn left up the road past thatched cottages before passing to the left of St Wynwallow church. Follow the road ahead past the school and back into Lizard village.

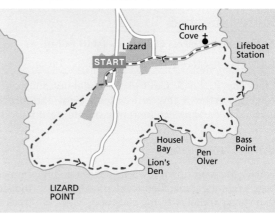

Moderate

WALK NO.

24

DISTANCE

3.5MILES

TIME

2.5HRS

MAP REF.

ORDNANCE SURVEY
LANDRANGER 203

704
126

COVERACK & LOWLAND POINT

Initial glimpses of the sea across farmland are an appetizer for the main course of this walk which is passage from above Lowland Point to the historic fishing and smuggling village of Coverack. Lowland Point is of interest to geographers as it is an example of a raised beach, formed when the sea level was once higher.

Offshore can be seen the start of the notorious Manacles Rocks which have claimed many ships. The 'John', an emigrant ship sailing from Plymouth to Canada sank here in 1855 with the loss of 196 lives; the 'Mohegan', a luxury liner, was lost in 1898 with 106 lives when it hit the Manacles at full speed.

Refreshments & Toilets

At Coverack. Toilets at car park (start point).

Directions to start

From the R.N.A.S. Culdrose roundabout south of Helston, take the B3293 towards St. Keverne. After a few miles, bear right and proceed on the B3294 into the village of Coverack. Parking can be found on the right hand side at the entrance to the village.

Walk Directions

Follow the road down towards the sea and bear left along a metalled residential lane that runs parallel with the coastline.

Immediately after the last house and where the lane becomes unmade, take a left hand track that leads to a stone stile and into woodland. Following yellow waymarks, continue through gorse and woodland, passing a grassy clearing to a wooden stile and some steps in the hedge.

Cross the field, bearing left on the obvious path, through a further clearing before bearing off to the left past rock outcrops. At the top, a lane with low stone walls and trees on either side leads ahead before bearing right. Pass across a field keeping to the left hand hedge and then on through two fields to pass a cattle pen on your right. Just past the cattle pen, cross over a stile which is adjacent to a metal gate and turn right down a concrete farm lane.

The lane eventually becomes unmade and passes through a farmyard before continuing ahead on a narrow track. Cross a stone stile and on through woods and a stream to reach a metalled lane that passes the thatched Trevalsoe Farm on the right.

Shortly after the farm, do not bear off left through a gate, instead continue ahead and cross a stile adjacent to a metal gate. Cross the field and over the wall stile ahead. Now walk straight ahead, keeping to the right hand side. Cross a stile next to a gate and then a field to a wooden stile adjacent to a farm track. Cross the next field to reach and cross a further stile in the opposite hedge boundary. Cross the next field ahead (rock outcrops and sea views here). A further stile and field are crossed, a large farm on the left. Cross two stiles and continue ahead, keeping to the left to cross a stone stile, heading

towards a further farm.

Continue just to the right of the corrugated farm building before passing through a left hand gate and following the track away from the farm on the right. A brown public footpath sign on the right should be followed to a kissing gate, the quarry buildings and pier becoming more visible on your left as you follow the path towards the sea. Offshore can be seen the start of the notorious Manacles Rocks.

Pass through a kissing gate, descending next to a metal handrail towards Lowland Point which is entered via a stile. After rounding the point Coverack can be seen in the distance. Follow the coastal path back to the village via stepping stones in areas prone to muddiness and using the occasional gate. Upon emerging onto a gravel track, turn left and follow the lane used earlier back to your car.

Moderate

WALK NO.
25

DISTANCE
4 MILES

TIME
2.5 HRS

MAP REF.
ORDNANCE SURVEY
LANDRANGER 204
782
187

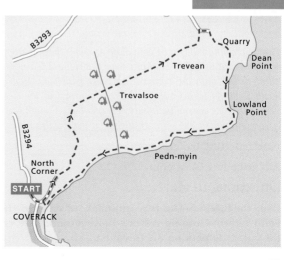

PORTHALLOW, GILLAN & NARE POINT

The tiny fishing village of Porthallow provides the starting point for a superb walk through woodland and farmland to Gillan Harbour near the Helford River estuary. In many ways however, the best is saved to last with an exhilarating coast path walk from Gillan around Nare Point and south to Porthallow; its white cottages a sharp contrast to the clear blue waters off this part of the Lizard Peninsula. The coastal path here is rarely busy though there is much to see and enjoy; the busy port of Falmouth often has ships at anchor in the bay as well as a flotilla of pleasure craft in the summer.

Refreshments & Toilets

At Porthallow (start point).

Directions to start

From the R.N.A.S. Culdrose roundabout south of Helston, take the B3293 to St. Keverne. Follow Porthallow signs from St. Keverne square, crossing the bridge over the stream in the village to park on the foreshore.

Walk Directions

From the car park, return to the main road, turn right and proceed ahead past both a phone box and the right turn to Manaccan. Continue ahead before bearing left over the stream. Just in front of a row of terraced cottages, turn right and head for a wooden kissing gate next to a farm gate. Take the path to a gate and keep on the lower path that starts to proceed up the valley.

A gradual climb (often muddy) passes up the left hand side of the valley, crossing en route a low stone wall and two boardwalks. The path bears left as it continues uphill passing over a stile next to a metal farm gate. Bearing to the right, adjacent to the hedge, cross a breeze block wall via steps next to a metal farm gate. This leads to a road upon which you should turn left, passing a farm on the right.

Follow the road ahead, eventually uphill to turn right at a T junction signed to Gillan. The narrow country road winds its way ahead between hedges with rolling countryside on either side. Pass the Gillan sign on the left and continue ahead to where the main road bears off to the left and a right hand side road is signed to Lestowder. Here, continue straight across following a concrete farm track, the views across to Falmouth Bay becoming ever clearer.

Pass the farm following the track past a new barn and up between hedges. Follow the lane and just before a metal barrier fence on the left, next to a clump of trees, pass through to descend on a

narrow woodland track which descends to Gillan Harbour.

At the bottom, notice a National Trust sign indicating The Herra. Pass to the right, up a grassy path that leads to a series of steps before bearing off left to follow the obvious coastal path. Excellent views are now afforded towards the Helford River estuary and Falmouth Bay, the latter often occupied by a number of large ships waiting at anchor.

It is now a case of following the coastal footpath back to Porthallow, proceeding around Nare Point with its observation post and onto Nare Head from where the tiny Porthallow village can be seen in the far distance.

Moderate

WALK NO.
26

DISTANCE
4.5 MILES

TIME
2.5 MILES

MAP REF.
ORDNANCE SURVEY
LANDRANGER 203
798
233

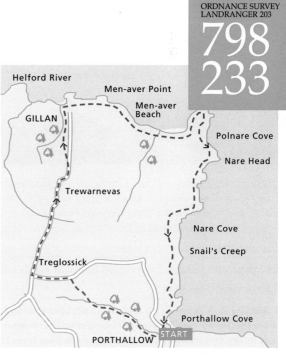

Helford River

Men-aver Point

Men-aver Beach

GILLAN

Polnare Cove

Nare Head

Trewarnevas

Nare Cove

Snail's Creep

Treglossick

Porthallow Cove

PORTHALLOW START

PORTSCATHO, TOWAN BEACH & ROSTEAGUE

The attractive fishing village of Portscatho on the Roseland Peninsula is the starting point for a lovely walk to the secluded National Trust cove of Towan Beach. Principal sea views take in Nare Head, and further up the coast, Dodman Point. Completion of the circuit is via quiet country lanes and fields bordered by crops of tulips and daffodils in springtime.

Refreshments & Toilets

In Portscatho village. Toilets also found at Porth Farm (N.T.) above Towan Beach.

Directions to start

From the A39 Truro to St. Austell road, take the A3078 signed to St. Mawes. Turn left just after the hamlet of Trewithian, signed to Portscatho. In approx. half a mile take a further left to the free car park for Porthcurnick Beach on the outskirts of Portscatho.

Walk Directions

Pass through a wooden gate at the lower right of the car park area signed to Portscatho village centre. Proceed into the village, turning left into the main road that runs above the harbour. Continue ahead until the road ends noting the splendid views to your left across Gerrans and Veryan Bays to Nare Head and Gull Rock and further up the coast to Dodman Point.

At this point, follow the path around to the right, climbing some steps onto the coastal path. Immediately after a stone stile, the path divides. Ignore the path to the left which leads to a small cove and continue ahead through a metal gate.

Follow the coastal path skirting fields and crossing stiles for approx. 1.5 miles before passing through a gate to enter the National Trust property of Towan Beach. Continue around just above the beach before turning right up a gravel track towards the National Trust buildings of Porth Farm (inc. toilets).

At the top of the track, pass through a gate and turn right onto a metalled road for about 20 yards only before taking the first track off to the right (private property on left) signed to Gerrans. As the track ascends, there are occasional glimpses left over Porth Creek which leads to the Percuil River.

Where the track departs to the left, continue straight on indicated by a signpost with a blue waymark arrow. Pass over a wooden stile, crossing the field towards a house ahead. A further stile and field leads to another stile accessing a driveway lane. Turn left and follow the quiet country lane ahead between open fields for about three quarters of a mile.

Pass a large farmhouse on the right before eventually reaching Treloan Farm. Find a footpath just afterwards on the right and walk down a sheltered track between hedges. Cross a stile at the end of this track to proceed diagonally across the field towards a corner of the hedge. From here, continue across the field in the same direction to reach the far left corner. At the corner of the field, cross a stile and descend via steps into Portscatho. On reaching the road, turn left for a short distance before turning right before the pub to proceed along North Parade (used earlier). Follow the lane ahead back up to the car park.

Moderate

WALK NO.

27

DISTANCE

4.5 MILES

TIME

2.5 HRS

MAP REF.

ORDNANCE SURVEY
LANDRANGER 204

878
358

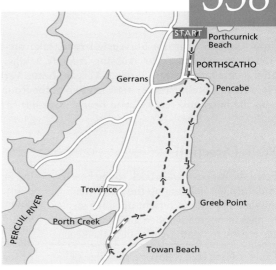

START Porthcurnick Beach

PORTHSCATHO

Gerrans

Pencabe

Trewince

Greeb Point

Porth Creek

PERCUIL RIVER

Towan Beach

NARE HEAD, GERRANS BAY & CARNE BEACON

The National Trust headland of Nare Head on the Roseland Peninsula with its stunning views across Gerrans Bay, is the main feature of this walk which commences from Carne Beach. The return is via open farmland and the historic village of Veryan, famous for its five thatched Round Houses. Shortly before the end of the walk the route passes the unusual Carne Beacon. This is Cornwall's largest tumulus and the believed burial site of a sixth century king called Geraint. Legend has it that his body was carried across Gerrans Bay on a golden boat with silver oars though archeological excavations have been unable to confirm this.

Refreshments & Toilets

Toilets (seasonal) in the NT car park at Carne Beach. Further toilets and pub etc. available in Veryan.

Directions to start

From the A39 Truro to St. Austell road, take the A3078 signed to St. Mawes. Follow A3078, turning right after crossing Tregony Bridge, eventually turning left immediately after a garage, to follow signs to Veryan. Leave Veryan by a lane (signed Pendower and Nare Head Hotel), passing between two of the Round Houses and follow narrow lane to pass the hotel and reach Carne Beach. Turn left in front of the beach to park in the car park.

Walk Directions

From the car park walk back to the beach and turn left heading up the hill. After only a few yards turn right up some steps to pass through a wooden gate and follow the coastal footpath overlooking the beach.

Cross a stone stile following the edge of the field to a wooden stile. Take the well defined coastal path towards Nare Head before crossing a wooden stile and descending to Paradoe Cove. Cross the stile and footbridge to ascend, with a disused stone building to your right. A further wooden stile is crossed just after a wooden bench, on the right near the top.

Continue straight ahead to reach a waymark post. Proceed to a fork from where a right turn leads to a path through the gorse bushes to the splendid viewpoint of Nare Head.

Retrace the route from Nare Head back to the coast path noting the large Gull Rock just offshore. Turn right to continue on the path skirting large gorse bushes ignoring the path leading off to the right through the gorse. At the corner of a wire fence, make your way along the obvious route through the gorse noting the outline of Dodman Point in the distance. Notice a green painted manhole about 3ft high.

Continue to the gate ahead, crossing a cattle grid onto a farm track and leaving the coastal path behind. The farm track skirts the edge of the field before exiting left over a cattle grid and passing a small National Trust parking area and the National Trust sign for Kiberick Cove.

From here proceed along the metalled road ahead. Pass a slate hung farm house and shortly afterwards, where the road bears around to the right in an 'S' bend, turn left up some slate steps in the hedge. (If you reach the sign for Caragloose Farm, you have gone too far). Keep to the left hand side to cross over a further stile in the hedge ahead.

Turn right, keeping the boundary of the field to your immediate right. After a short distance, turn left across the field to pass through a metal gate. Turn right and keeping the field boundary on your right walk to the top right corner of the field. Pass over a step stile onto the road. Turn left on the road and head for the farm buildings. At the 'S' bend

cross wooden stile on right, next to a gate. Cross the field in the direction of a tree that appears to be at the left hand edge of the hedge and pass over stone stile to right of tree.

Continue diagonally across the field keeping telegraph pole well to your right. A stone stile in the hedge at the bottom of the field leads to a path adjacent to a wire fence. Head for the gate at the bottom right of the field situated by some houses. At the main road turn left. Leaving Veryan village behind, continue past a large farm house on the left to take a left turn across a stone stile and follow a public footpath signed to Carne.

Once in the field, proceed with the hedge to your immediate left, continuing around the field boundary before leaving via a stile next to a wooden gate. Do not proceed onto the lane, instead cross a stone and wooden stile on your immediate left. Cross the field keeping Carne Beacon (a tree covered hillock) to your left before leaving via a stone stile into a lane. Turn right down the lane and return to Carne Beach and your car.

Moderate

WALK NO.

28

DISTANCE

5 MILES

TIME

3 HRS

MAP REF.

ORDNANCE SURVEY LANDRANGER 204

905 383

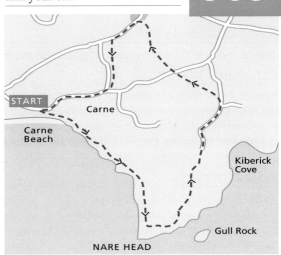

61

VERYAN, PORTLOE & THE JACKA

The delightful fishing village of Portloe is the halfway point on a four mile circular ramble across typical Cornish farmland to the coastal path overlooking Veryan Bay. From Portloe the walk follows the coast path to Broom Parc, the National Trust property used in the filming of 'The Camomile Lawn.' Quiet country lanes and a stretch of woodland returns you to the historic village of Veryan with its picturesque church and much photographed Round Houses.

Refreshments & Toilets

Toilets, pub and shop at Veryan. Hotel restaurant, tearooms, pub and toilets in Portloe.

Directions to start

From the A39 Truro to St. Austell road, take the A3078 signed to St. Mawes. Continue on the A3078 over Tregony Bridge before eventually turning left immediately after a garage to follow signs to Veryan. There are a number of roadside parking opportunities in the village near to Veryan Parish Hall (opposite the pond gardens).

Walk Directions

At the memorial gardens next to the church, take the pondside public footpath indicated Portloe via Trewortha. Pass through a kissing gate and through the playing fields, leaving top right across a stream and a stone stile. Cross the field diagonally to the right of two large trees aiming for the top corner of the field. A

Walk Directions

small metal gate leads to a stone stile and a footpath through a copse. After a further stone stile, cross the field and head for the distant farm buildings.

Pass through a metal farm gate and follow the farm track past the Trewortha Holiday Apartments. At the road junction, turn left and then first right following a tarmac lane (public footpath sign indicating Portloe).

Continue along the lane between some houses and on between hedges noting the outline of Dodman Point ahead in the distance. The lane bears around to the right to the middle of farm buildings; here turn sharp left indicated by the yellow footpath arrow(metal farm gate). A track leads down between these farm buildings and on between hedges, eventually reaching two adjacent metal gates. Pass through the left hand gate and proceed ahead with the hedge to your immediate right.

Descend to cross stone steps in the hedge on the right before bearing right diagonally across the field to a metal gate in the corner that leads on to what appears to be a private driveway next to some houses. Bear right out of this close to turn sharp left onto the main road, descending into the attractive fishing village of Portloe.

At the harbour, next to the Post Office and tea rooms, take the right hand path passing the public toilets and ascend to rejoin the coastal path. Continue to a path junction, bearing left indicated by the yellow waymark arrow. The coastal path continues

through gorse and blackthorn bushes with Gull Rock clearly in view offshore.

Cross a wooden stile to follow the coastal path as it heads towards the large white property at Broom Parc. Cross a further wooden stile to descend via steps and on past some pine trees. Where the path rises to meet another path, turn sharp right, leaving the coast path, to follow the track past Broom Parc and on to a road.

Continue on the road ahead towards the hamlet of Camels until reaching a cross roads. Continue straight over (signed Veryan 3/4 mile). After approximately 300 yards at a row of trees, turn right on to a public footpath. Cross a wooden stile and turn left to follow the hedge boundary. Pass over a further wooden stile to descend through the woodland, exiting via a wooden stile into the field used earlier on the walk. Turn left, returning to your car via the childrens' playground and memorial gardens.

Moderate

WALK NO.

29

DISTANCE

4 MILES

TIME

2 HRS

MAP REF.

ORDNANCE SURVEY
LANDRANGER 204

916
397

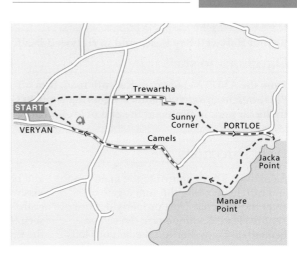

PORTH JOKE, KELSEY HEAD & HOLYWELL BAY

This walk encounters some striking contrasts within the landscape of a short section of the north Cornwall coast. From West Pentire Head with its views up the Gannel Estuary to the dunes of Crantock Beach, the coast path leads to the quiet charm of Porth (or locally Polly) Joke, a scenic beach popular with those seeking to escape the crowds of nearby Newquay. The route leads out onto the rocky promonotory of Kelsey Head, used extensively by nesting seabirds, before passing through mountainous sand dunes at Holywell Bay. The distinctive twin peaks of Carter's Rocks are just offshore. The final part of the walk returns via the Kelseys, a series of ancient field enclosures now in the care of the National Trust.

Refreshments & Toilets

Behind Holywell Bay Beach and in Holywell itself.

Directions to start

From the A3075 Newquay to Redruth road, turn off signed to Crantock and West Pentire. Pass straight through Crantock (ignoring signs to Crantock village and beach) and park in the car park indicated at the end of West Pentire village.

Walk Directions

From the car park, return to the main road and turn left passing through a gate to enter the National Trust property of West Pentire Head. Continue past the signed footpath to Polly (Porth) Joke on your left, and bear right at a gate, passing through a kissing gate to descend onto the coastal path. To the right over the hedge can be seen the sand dunes of Crantock Beach and the River Gannel estuary. At a path junction, keep left, following the grassy coastal footpath to the end of West Pentire Head.

From the headland, the footpath passes around the delightful sandy cove of Porth Joke and onto the next headland, Kelsey Head. The Chick Island lies just off shore. The sound of gunfire can sometimes be heard here and originates from the military training installation at Penhale Point, to the south of Holywell Bay.

Leaving Kelsey Head behind, pass through a gate to follow the path as it skirts cliffs above Holywell Bay (at this point can be seen the twin peaks of the Carters or Gull Rocks, just offshore). After a further gate, follow the boardwalk path through the sand dunes and down onto the beach.

Turn left as soon as you step on to the beach and almost immediately turn left again where there is a fairly wide gap in the sand dunes. You will now continue along a sand path and within a few yards the path divides. Take the right path which has a part board walk.

Shortly afterwards, the path bears right and brings you to a stream with a sand clearing. Take the left sand path leading towards houses (Holywell) which brings you on to a metalled path (yellow acorn sign indicating Holywell). Continue up this metalled path for a few yards and then turn very sharp left to walk along a path with bungalows on your right. Keep right.

Head once again into the dunes, following the rather steep sandy path next to a wire fence. Follow

the path to the left of the golf course boundary. The sandy path climbs adjacent to the golf course before passing through a gate onto the open grassy expanse of the Kelseys. Continue ahead to reach a gate next to the end of the golf course. Pass through the gate and turn sharp left to continue ahead with the wire fence now on your immediate left. Where the fence turns off left, continue straight on to reach a track leading from the large white house above right.

At the track, turn left and proceed to the bottom of the valley, passing a National Trust path with a sign on a gate to Polly Joke. Follow the path partially around to the right to find a kissing gate (next to Polly Joke camp site). The path follows a wall before crossing a stream and turning left up a steep track eventually leading back to the car.

WALK NO.

30

DISTANCE

4.5 MILES

TIME

2.5 HRS

MAP REF.

ORDNANCE SURVEY
LANDRANGER 200

777 605

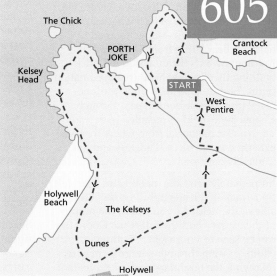

PADSTOW, STEPPER POINT & THE CAMEL ESTUARY

From the picturesque fishing harbour of Padstow, this walk crosses open farmland before reaching the coastal path. The isolated Butter Hole Cove with its multicoloured rock strata is passed before reaching Pepper Hole, a collapsed sea cave. After rounding the headland of Stepper Point with its distinctive beacon, this walk provides superb views across the stunning Camel Estuary. The beauty of the beaches passed at Harbour Cove and St. George's Well contrasts with the danger of the notorious Doom Bar, the sand bank at the approach to the estuary responsible for claiming many ships and lives.

Refreshments & Toilets

Toilets in car park at start point. Refreshments and all facilities in Padstow.

Directions to start

Park in the top Padstow car park, signed from the A389, the town's main approach road.

Walk Directions

Pass through the gap in the car park boundary in the direction of the town centre. Go through the children's play area, turning left and descending steps to a lane. Turn right before heading left down a further lane indicating the town centre via steps. At the bottom of the steps, bear right before turning left to follow the road to the harbour. Bear left in front of the harbour, heading towards the quayside red brick building that houses the tourist information centre. Shortly after here climb the lane away from the harbour to pass through Chapel Style field. A metalled path leads up to a war memorial from where there are extensive views across Padstow and the Camel Estuary.

Immediately after the metal gates, turn left up a track that leads uphill on the left hand side of the field. As you climb, the mouth of the estuary and the infamous Doom Bar can be seen to your right. Continue to climb, passing through a large farm gate, following the boundary wall of Prideaux Place Deerpark on your left. A metal gate leads on to a road.

Turn right and walk ahead for nearly 500 yards to find a public footpath sign on the left adjacent to a slate stile. Cross the field diagonally, following a track to reach a second stile. Cross the field heading for a post in the opposite hedge located between two telegraph poles. Cross a third stile to enter a small field that leads to stile four. Cross the large arable field diagonally towards the top end of a line of telegraph poles. A fifth stile allows passage across a further field to stile six, again following the direction of the telegraph poles that head towards farm buildings. After stile seven, continue towards the farm buildings before finally passing over an eighth stile, next to a metal gate, that leads to a gravel track.

Bear left between cottages before turning right onto a road. Follow the road ahead (ignore a left bearing road), Trevose Head can be seen over the hedge on your left.

The road gently descends before bearing away to the right. Follow the road right for approximately 100 yards before turning left to cross a stile. This leads to a path up the side of the field and past a wire fence to reach the coastal path.

Turn right and follow the path leading to the beacon on Stepper Point that can be seen in the distance. A kissing gate and a stone stile are encountered before reaching the dramatic Butter Hole with its multi coloured rocks. Pass through the kissing gate here to round Butter Hole and onto the collapsed sea cave of Pepper Hole.

On reaching the beacon, continue ahead (a short cut goes right towards the old coastguard lookout), rounding Stepper Point to reach a wooden stile. The Doom Bar sands that have claimed so many lives over the years can now be seen on the approach to the estuary. The path bears right adjacent to a fence before reaching a wooden kissing gate and descending in the direction of a row of houses.

A wooden kissing gate leads to the houses at Hawker's Cove. Follow the metalled road before bearing left on the bend to rejoin the coastal path. Cross a stile to pass behind the old lifeboat building and continue ahead towards the sandy beach at Harbour Cove. Pass over a stile and follow the path around to the right. Descend via steps before crossing a wooden boardwalk following the waymark arrows.

A small copse leads to a wooden stile before bearing left to follow

a path at the bottom of the field. Cross a further stile on the left and follow a path over a boardwalk before bearing right. Shortly afterwards, turn left and follow the field edge before crossing left over a stile to skirt a further field. Another stile should be crossed before leaving Harbour Cove behind and proceeding through a gap next to a large stile and onto a distinct track that leads past Gun Point.

The track descends to round the beach at St. George's Well before following the well made track back to the war memorial. Proceed back through Chapel Style field to the harbour.

From the harbour, retrace your steps back to your car by turning right into The Strand and then left and a further left signed to Wadebridge. Just before the road climbs away, turn right into Mill Road and back up the steps to the car park.

Moderate

WALK NO.

31

DISTANCE

6 MILES

TIME

3.5 HRS

MAP REF.

ORDNANCE SURVEY
LANDRANGER 200

915
754

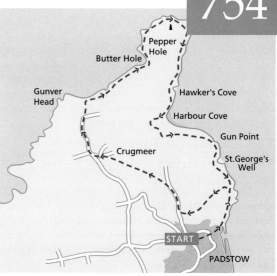

PENTIRE POINT & RUMPS POINT

The headland of Pentire Point and Rumps Point is one of a series of promontories on this part of the north coast. Close by are Stepper Point and Trevose Head, both of which can clearly be seen in the first half of the walk. The circuit departs from above the sheltered family beach of Hayle Bay to round Pentire Point, of interest to geologists as a pumice stone like rock called Pillow Lava is found here. From Pentire Point it is only a short walk to the magnificent Rumps headland, previously used as an Iron Age cliff castle, the earthwork ditches from which are still clearly visible. A walk back across N.T. farmland returns you to the start point.

Refreshments & Toilets

Toilets next to car park at start point in New Polzeath. Beach shops and cafes at Polzeath.

Directions to start

From the northern end of Wadebridge by-pass, follow the Wadebridge sign before turning right at the first roundabout onto the B3314. Follow the signs for Polzeath and shortly after the Porteath Bee Centre, turn right for New Polzeath, parking in the main car park. (A limited number of free parking spaces are also available overlooking the sea).

Walk Directions

Leave the car park via the steps next to the toilet block and turn right into Gulland Road. At the end of the road, before it bears around to the left, take the coastal path opposite. Pass around the picturesque cove of Pentireglaze Haven and through a wooden gate to enter the National Trust property of Pentire and Pentireglaze.

After a short distance, the path divides. Do not turn right to Pentire Farm, instead bear left keeping to the coastal path. Views from the headland include Stepper Point with its 'pepperpot' daymark and Trevose Head and lighthouse. The attractive beach and dunes to the south of Stepper Point at Harbour Cove, are reached on foot from Padstow town centre via the War Memorial and St. George's Well Cove.

Continue on the obvious coastal path to the rocky outcrop of Pentire Point, Newland Rock can be seen offshore. From Pentire Point, continue on the headland's coastal path whereupon the next destination of Rumps Point, eventually comes into view. Where the path divides into two, take the lower path bearing left to Rumps Point. A path created by Iron Age inhabitants passes through a series of ditches to the twin peaks of the headland. The summit to the left is the more obvious target though there are paths to and between both points of the headland.

Turning back from the Rumps, cross the neck of the peninsula, keeping on the broad path straight ahead to a gate. Continue with the wall to your right until a junction of stone walls is reached. Turn right through a gate signed to Pentire Farm keeping the hedge to your immediate left. At the top of the rise, with Stepper Point once more visible, turn left along a farm track and proceed through the yard at Pentire Farm. Opposite the slate hung farmhouse, turn right through a gate indicating the coastal path.

Descend to the path junction used earlier, bearing left up some steps to retrace the route around Pentireglaze Haven and back to your car.

Moderate

WALK NO.

32

DISTANCE

3.5 MILES

TIME

2 HRS

MAP REF.

ORDNANCE SURVEY
LANDRANGER 200

937
797

69

GORRAN HAVEN & DODMAN POINT

Dodman Point is one of Cornwall's most spectacular headlands and offers stunning views across Veryan Bay towards Nare Head. The Dodman's defensive capabilities were recognised and enhanced by Iron Age Man who built a massive earthwork fortification here. This is known as the 'Bulwark' and consisted of a tall bank of earth above a deep ditch. This offered the settlement protection from the one side open to attack (tall sea cliffs secured the other three sides). Part of this walk passes through the ditch of the 'Bulwark' and along with a large stone cross on the headland, affords added interest to the superb views.

Prior to reaching the Dodman, you pass the rarely crowded Vault Beach, its west facing sands providing an excellent spot for picnics on sunny days.

Refreshments & Toilets

Both available within Gorran Haven village.

Directions to start

From the double mini roundabout on the A390 in St Austell, follow the B3273 signed to Mevagissey. After Pentewan, turn right at the top of the hill indicating Gorran Haven (6 miles). Proceed through Gorran High Lanes and Gorran Churchtown to Gorran Haven. Descend into the village and park in the large car park signed on the left.

Walk Directions

From the car park, turn left and proceed to the harbour, passing a toilet block on the right. Turn right shortly before the beach up Foxhole Lane and climb some steps indicating a public footpath. Pass through a kissing gate and ascend with the harbour and beach below you on the left. Cross a stile and a kissing gate and follow the obvious coastal path. A little after a stone bench, the path divides. Keep left, down some stone steps, taking the lower path above the gull nesting sites to pass around Maenease Point. After a short distance, the imposing mass of Dodman Point appears before you.

Where the path forks, keep right (acorn sign) and climb to a kissing gate, continuing on the coastal path with Vault Beach below to your left. Head over a complex wooden stile next to a National Trust sign indicating you have just passed through Lamledra and make your way through a small copse.

From the copse, continue along the path, crossing two wooden stiles before coming to a path junction. Turn left signed to Dodman Point. Two further wooden stiles are crossed before you arrive at the granite cross which looks out across Veryan Bay to Nare Head. From the cross, at the acorn post, turn sharp left and walk for about a quarter of a mile to a wooden stile. Turn right on a public footpath signed to Penare. You are now walking in the ditch of the 'Bulwark', part of a massive iron age fortification constructed to defend an Iron Age settlement.

Follow the main track ahead, passing through a gate to reach a metalled road. Turn right, passing some stone properties. Continue uphill to where the road bears around to the left and is joined by a road from the right. At this junction, continue ahead through a wooden gate indicating a public footpath to Treveague. The small church tower of Gorran Churchtown can be seen in the

distance. Proceed ahead adjacent to the wire fence passing through a metal gate and continuing straight ahead.

Pass through a second metal gate where there is a signpost to Treveague. Keep straight ahead across the field to go through a wooden gate. Turn sharp right signed to Gorran Haven. Pass Treveague Farm before bearing immediate left to follow a yellow waymark post. Pass Treveague (on your right) and bear left through a metal gate (signed to Gorran Haven) immediately pass through a wooden gate. Continue downhill and where the path forks, bear right to a kissing gate to follow stepping stones behind some houses. After a wooden gate, follow the lane to the main road, turning right to return to the car park.

Moderate

WALK NO.
33

DISTANCE
4 MILES

TIME
2 HRS

MAP REF.
ORDNANCE SURVEY LANDRANGER 204
012 416

GORRAN HAVEN
START
Maenease Point
Bow or Vault Beach
Penare
Penveor Point
DODMAN POINT

Mevagissey, an archetypal Cornish fishing village, draws large numbers of visitors throughout the year. The development of the harbour area loved by tourists today was as a result of prosperity brought by pilchards, the catch salted in deep barrels on the quayside and exported in vast quantities to Mediterranean countries. The port was well known for building fast sailing boats called luggers which were popular with Cornish smugglers along the whole of the south coast.

As well as climbing above the village to allow views across the busy harbour, this walk also has far reaching vistas to the promontories of Black Head and Gribbin Head that mark the limits of St. Austell Bay. After turning inland, the walk follows well used paths through woodland and open countryside before returning back to Mevagissey where there are ample opportunities for refreshment.

Refreshments & Toilets

Both in Mevagissey at the start of the walk.

Directions to start

From the double mini roundabout on the A390 in St. Austell, take the B3273 signed to Mevagissey. Park in the car and coach park on the left at the entrance to the village. In winter when this car park is closed, park in one of the smaller car parks and walk through Mevagissey to the harbour.

Walk Directions

Walk down to the harbour. Standing with your back to the Sharksfin Hotel and restaurant, walk down the left hand side of the harbour towards Mevagissey Museum.

Shortly after passing a toilet block, turn sharp left up a steep lane in front of cottages and then turn right at a junction to pass in front of a property with a large anchor on the wall. The path climbs to reveal the view right across the outer harbour and runs up steps to pass in front of a shelter and seating. After the coastguard lookout, a few steps lead into a recreation field. Continue ahead to leave the field via a gap just below some houses (the view is across Black Head to St. Austell Bay).

The path continues along the bottom of gardens, over a granite step stile before descending to a stile. A boardwalk is negotiated before bearing left to climb steps. Emerge into a field, walking past a bench and continue on the right hand side. Over a wooden stile and in the far distance Gribbin Head with its daymark tower used by ships for navigation. Walk around the edge of fields, gaining height before crossing a wooden stile. Shortly afterwards is a further stile with steps down to a further stile. The coastal path rounds Penare Point to reveal Pentewan Beach before you.

Cross the stile which overlooks Pentewan Beach, and walk, keeping to the right hand side, down the hill. Cross two wooden stiles before following the coastal path up the side of Portgiskey Cove where there are some remains of ruined buildings. A wooden stile leads you right to pass over two further stiles close together. A boardwalk is also encountered. Now leave the coastal path (which bears right)

and walk straight ahead uphill on a well defined steep path. At the top, cross a stile and turn left along a footpath. Follow the path through parking spaces alongside the road. On reaching a crossroads, turn right and cross the road (signed to Gorran Haven and The Lost Gardens of Heligan).

Continue along the road past a lengthy stretch of concrete wall. After passing a road on the right, walk for approximately 150 yards and opposite a view to your right across Pentewan, cross the road left to a wooden stile (near an electricity sub station). Over the stile, and follow the track to meet the coast and clay trail/cycle path in front of you. The woods on your right are part of Heligan estate. Walk ahead and on past granite posts into a small wood and through a second set of granite posts before descending downhill. At the tarmac lane continue past a football pitch to the main road. Pass a children's play area and walk back to Mevagissey and the car park.

Moderate

WALK NO.
34

DISTANCE
IN MILES
4

TIME
IN HOURS
2.5

MAP REF.
ORDNANCE SURVEY
LANDRANGER 204
013
450

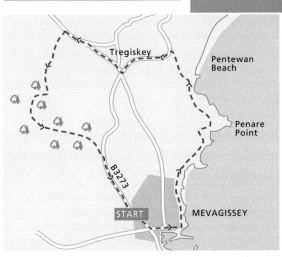

POLKERRIS & GRIBBIN HEAD

Gribbin Head is a classic Cornish headland most suitable for the creation of a circular coastal walk. A long, fairly level coastline heads south before turning north to return to the start point having made only a relatively small usage of road.

From the pretty bathing cove of Polkerris, the walk passes above a coastline along which can usually be seen cormorants and shags. After rounding The Gribbin with its distinctive red and white striped daymark, the route turns inland to pass close to Menabilly. This was the one time home of Daphne du Maurier who used it as the setting for three of her novels including that of Manderley in 'Rebecca'.

Refreshments & Toilets

Inn, beach shop and toilets at Polkerris (start point).

Directions to start

From the A390 Truro to St. Austell road, take the A3082 signed to Fowey adjacent to the Cornish Marketworld retail development. Pass the Par China Clay works, following the Par one way system and signs for Fowey. Proceed out of Polmear for about a mile before turning right, signed to Polkerris. Take the first right, a car park is on the right hand side.

Walk Directions

Turn right out of the car park and walk down the lane to enjoy the views across St. Austell Bay from the unspoilt beach at Polkerris. The Rashleigh Inn and a beach shop are located here.

Proceed back up the road from the Rashleigh Inn for 30 yards before turning right to walk up towards a toilet block. Follow the track past the toilets to reach a fork, where a black and white cottage inscribed "JCSR" is located. Walk up the incline (left) and follow steps right adjacent to a waymark post and acorn sign.

Continue along a path which meanders up through a wooded glade. At the end of the wood turn right, following the edge of a field. Cross a wooden stile. Clear views of Par China Clay Docks to the right and views across St. Austell Bay, Black Head and Mevagissey Bay leading to Dodman Point can be seen from this part of the route.

Continue on the path across 5 gates & stiles, before reaching a sign marking the National Trust property of The Gribbin. Where the track forks, both paths lead to Gribbin Head Tower, erected in 1832 by the Trinity House Association, which is open to the public on certain days of the year.

Follow the path downhill away from the tower, fine views of Polridmouth Cove and Fowey estuary can be seen ahead. Carry on this path, leaving Gribbin Head by a wooden gate and follow the path towards Polridmouth Cove. After crossing a boardwalk above a secluded cove, pass through a gate on the

left and climb away from the sea following a gravel track.

The track widens before passing Menabilly Barton Farm, assuming a metalled lane to a metal gate. Follow the road ahead passing occasional houses to reach Tregaminion Church after approx. 1/2 mile. Shortly after the church is a waymark post on the left hand side. The unusual symbol, the stylised cross, indicates you are now walking on part of the Saints Way, an ancient path between Padstow and Fowey used by traders and pilgrims for perhaps thousands of years.

Continue along the road for a short distance to find a path signpost on the left. Take this path and walk ahead. Reach the wooded glade encountered at the start of the walk and follow the zig zag path downhill through the trees. Now follow the route used earlier back to your car.

Moderate

WALK NO.
35

DISTANCE
3.5 MILES

TIME
2 HRS

MAP REF.
ORDNANCE SURVEY
LANDRANGER 203
094
524

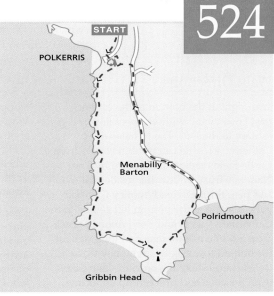

READYMONEY COVE & ST CATHERINE'S CASTLE

The delightfully named Readymoney Cove is the starting point for a short walk that starts along the ancient Saints Way, a route used for centuries by pilgrims and traders travelling between Padstow on the north coast and Fowey on the south. After passing through Covington Woods and across National Trust farmland, the attractive Polridmouth Cove with its ornamental lake (and swans) is reached. The coastal path return via Lankelly Cliff and Alldays Fields provides superb vistas over the busy entrance to Fowey harbour.

The remains of St. Catherine's Castle, one of a series of forts constructed by Henry VIII, and the Rashleigh Mausoleum, dedicated to a 19th century landowning family, are situated at the end of the walk and are freely open to visitors.

Refreshments & Toilets

Toilets at start point car park. Toilets and refreshments (in season) at Readymoney Cove. Many facilities in nearby Fowey.

Directions to start

From the A390 Truro to St Austell road, take the A3082 signed to Fowey adjacent to the Cornish Marketworld retail development. Pass the Par China Clay works, following the Par one way system and signs for Fowey. At Fowey, follow signs to the main and beach car and coach park, off Hanson Drive.

Walk Directions

Turn right at the bottom of the car park, past Fowey Hall with views of Fowey estuary to the left. The remains of St. Catherine's Castle can be seen clearly from Castle Fields viewpoint, owned by The National Trust. Follow the residential road and pass through Readymoney Cove car park, leaving at the bottom left signed to St. Catherine's Castle and Readymoney Beach. Turn left into a leafy lane and then right at the bottom towards Readymoney Cove (toilets here). Take the far right lane away from the cove and proceed up an incline,

stopping briefly to read about The Saints Way, marked with its own unique sign, the stylised cross. Climb past the National Trust sign indicating Covington Woods to where the path forks next to a stone post. Turn left up steps and climb to a metal kissing gate.

Keep to the right hand edge of the field and after only a few yards pass through a gap in the boundary. Head diagonally across the field, the red and white striped daymark on Gribbin Head is off to your left. Pass over a stile next to a metal gate and follow the track to Coombe Farm. Walk to the end of the lane, passing the farm house on your left to reach a junction.

Take the second left (the first leads into the National Trust car park) and head down a lane with the Gribbin daymark directly in front of you. Follow the lane to the right, reaching a gate. Pass through the gate and across the field via an obvious track. Follow a footpath arrow that descends before bearing left to provide views over Polridmouth Cove. Pass through a wooden gate and down a well worn lane that descends through light woodland and a wooden gate, next to a large metal gate. A further metal gate at the bottom leads to Polridmouth Cove.

Turn left and proceed up the track marked as National Trust Lankelly Cliff. Steps lead to a wooden stile, the coastal path climbing to a wooden gate before descending to provide views up the Fowey estuary. The remains of the Polruan blockhouse can be seen on the estuary's eastern approach. Pass over a small boardwalk and a stile at the head of a small cove. Follow the path around to the right descending over a wooden stile to reach the National Trust property of Coombe Haven.

Climb up out of Coombe, across a wooden stile, following the track around towards Fowey, marked by a stone pillar detailing "Alldays Fields'. Pass through a kissing gate and follow a track that leads off right around the headland to reach the National

Trust property of St. Catherine's Point. Bear left and for the moment pass the sign to St. Catherine's Castle, and reach a path junction. Here bear left up a track for a short distance. At a further path junction, turn left and immediately sharp left again up an incline to visit the fairly overgrown Rashleigh Mausoleum.

From here, return to the sign for St. Catherine's Castle and take time to explore the English Heritage maintained remains (free admittance).

Retrace your steps to the St. Catherine's Castle signpost and bear right down steps to follow the path leading to Readymoney Cove. Proceed out of the cove, at toilet block turn right and walk up hill to the lane on the left marked "St. Catherine's Parade" along which you would have earlier walked. Return to your car through Readymoney Cove car park and on to Fowey car park via Hanson Drive.

Moderate

WALK NO.

36

DISTANCE

3.5 MILES

TIME

2 HRS

MAP REF.
ORDNANCE SURVEY
LANDRANGER 200

114
517

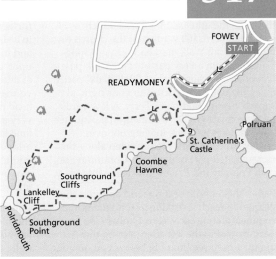

FOWEY, BODINNICK, PONT & POLRUAN

The River Fowey is one of Cornwall's most attractive and important rivers. Legions of small pleasure craft and sailing boats are moored here and you can sometimes see the large cargo ships being guided by tugs to the china clay loading bays above the Bodinnick Ferry.

This walk commences via a pedestrian ferry crossing of the river to allow you to reach the start of the 'Hall Walk'. This provides, quite simply, some of the best river and estuary views you are likely to find. The walk continues alongside the lush wooded creek of Pont Pill before climbing past the ancient church of Lanteglos to reach the coast path. Stunning sea views are available all the way back to Polruan from where a further passenger ferry provides the return to Fowey through which you walk back to your car.

Do not be put off by the need to use pedestrian ferries for this walk. The cost is very low and the views far too stunning to miss.

Refreshments & Toilets

Toilets near the Bodinnick Ferry and at Polruan. Pubs, restaurant & tea rooms at Fowey and Polruan.

Directions to start

From the A390 between St. Austell and St. Blazey Gate, take the A3082 signed to Par. From Par follow signs to Fowey until reaching a crossroads. Take the B3269 signed Bodinnick Ferry (Looe) and park in the car park adjacent to the ferry. The ferry operates daily until dusk all the year round.

Walk Directions

From the car park, cross the ferry as a foot passenger. Walk up the hill from the slipway past the Old Ferry Inn. On the right just past the inn is the unusual St. John's Church, a converted barn. 100 yards past the church turn right into Hall Walk marked Polruan 4 miles. Continuing on a very narrow lane walk past a National Trust sign marked 'Hall Walk' partly along the path. Look down to your right, a superb view of Bodinnick Ferry. A few yards further on is a granite war memorial. Another outstanding view here looking out over Fowey. Wooden seats are provided along this very wooded part of the walk. Continuing on, both Polruan and Fowey now come into view.

Pass a shelter with seating (and an interesting plaque) to reach a striking granite memorial commemorating Sir Arthur Quiller Couch. Bear around to the left after passing the monument to see Pont Pill below you on your right. Continue up the side of Pont Pill to pass over a stile which marks the end of the National Trust property. About 100 yards further on turn right through a gate adjacent to a slate stile descending on a rather steep and in places rocky path. You then come upon a sign marked Polruan, turn sharp right at this point almost doubling back on yourself. This path now leads down to the head of Pont Pill. At the head of this creek is a very attractive house with a well preserved lime kiln adjacent to it. Cross the wooden bridge towards the house, noticing on the house a sign dated 1894 giving the dues required for discharging items such as grain, timber, manure, sand etc.

Continue straight on past the house and climb up the path passing Pont Creek Farmhouse and Pont Creek Cottage on your right. A few yards past these houses you come to a sign 'Footpath to Polruan' which is to your right. Ignore this and continue straight up the fairly steep path to climb up some stone steps. At the top of the steps you come to a road, turn left for a few yards to arrive at a gate on your right marked 'footpath to church'.

Go through the gate and climb between trees, passing through a white gate to enter the cemetery of the very fine Lanteglos Church with its imposing tower. Walk up the path in front of the church and through a white gate, turn left out of the church and down the hill, passing Churchtown Farm on your right. Keeping to the road, continue up the hill.

At the top of the hill pass the N.T. Pencarrow car park on your left. On reaching the main road, cross to the far side and enter a gate immediately facing you to follow a clearly marked path on your right running parallel to the road. At the end of the path pass through another wooden gate and turn left, walking uphill through a field keeping close to the hedge on your left.

After about 300 yards you will come to a gate. Turn right before the gate and descend with hedge on the left. From this point there is a lovely view of Lantic Bay with Pencarrow Head just to your left and the pleasant Lantic Beach just below you. Proceeding along the coastal path you begin to climb quite steeply. Go through a gate at the western end of Lantic Bay and continue past a bench and a N.T. collection box. Walk on to the highest point from where there are impressive views up the coastline.

After a gate, comes a fairly steep descent. Follow the coast path ahead through three gates and over a stile. As you near the Fowey estuary, you can see a the red and white beacon of Gribbin Head on the opposite side. The coast path finally bears right to a large wooden farm gate that leads on to the road. Turn left and follow the sign towards the car park. Pass the school on your right and a terrace of houses to reach a tremendous vantage point up the Fowey estuary. Turn right on a path that descends down between gardens and houses into Polruan itself, marked village and harbour.

The ferry from the quay at Polruan runs frequently and will drop you at Whitehouse Point near the Fowey Hotel on the esplanade (this is during the summer every day until 11pm and winter time until 7pm weekdays, 5pm Sundays operating from Town Quay in the centre of Fowey). To complete the walk, make your way along the esplanade into Fowey. Keeping the Fowey Estuary to your right continue through the narrow streets of the town and back to the car park at Bodinnick Ferry.

Moderate

WALK NO.
37

DISTANCE
5 MILES

TIME
3 HRS

MAP REF.
ORDNANCE SURVEY
LANDRANGER 200
126 522

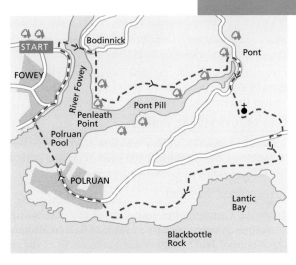

LANSALLOS & PENCARROW HEAD

Only a short distance from the bustle of Fowey to the west and Polperro to the east, this part of the south east Cornwall coast path offers a relative seclusion and peace that is enhanced by the views across Lantic and Lantivet Bays. It was this seclusion that once made the coastline here a favourite of smugglers with numerous coves suitable for the beaching of brandy, tea, rum and tobacco.

Much of the coastline in this area is under the protection of the National Trust including Pencarrow Head, "given anonymously in 1959 by a lover of Cornwall" ('Properties of the National Trust').

From Lansallos church, the walk crosses farmland before following the course of the minor road between Polruan and Polperro. After reaching the coastal path above Pencarrow Head, the route passes around Lantivet Bay before returning to Lansallos via a wooded track.

Refreshments & Toilets

Toilets in Lansallos village (close to start point). Further toilets available at the National Trust Frogmore car park, a 100 yard diversion from the main route of the walk. National Trust Tea Rooms in Lansallos (seasonal).

Directions to start

From the Crumplehorn roundabout at Polperro (the end of the A387), follow signs to Lansallos. Narrow country lanes lead to a small hamlet dominated by its church. Park in the National Trust car park 200 yards north of the church.

Walk Directions

Turn left out of the car park and proceed down the road towards the church. Immediately before the church gate, climb steps in a wall on your right to head across a field to a stile keeping the church wall on your left. Cross the stile and at the end of the wall, head across the field diagonally in the direction of farm buildings. Cross a stile and a wooden boardwalk into a second field, keeping to the left.

Descend to pass through two small gates into a small area of woodland. Ignore the left fork to Lansallos valley and descend steps to cross a small stream before ascending via a grassy track to a wooden gate. Continue ahead through the middle of the field (farm buildings on right). Pass beside a granite scratching post to reach stone steps in the field boundary before you.

Descend steps to a metalled lane and turn left. After about a third of a mile you reach a road junction (if toilets are required, turn right to reach the National Trust car park at Frogmore). Ignore the adjacent coastal path sign and follow the road left in the direction of Polruan.

Pass the National Trust properties at Triggabrowne and past the road that leads to their car park for Lantic Bay. Opposite this road is a coastal path sign on the left indicating Lantic Bay. Cross the stile and head up the field keeping the hedge on your left. As you pass over the rise, the National Trust headland can be seen jutting out below you between Lantic and Lantivet Bays.

Pass through a gate bearing left to pass a bench. The path forks

shortly before a rocky knoll. Follow the right hand path to enjoy vistas across the sheltered Lantic Bay, below to your right. After passing a wooden bench, the path reaches a path junction. Bear left and descend quite steeply to reach the coastal path leading around Lantivet Bay. Cross a wooden gate and enjoy a usually peaceful and relaxing walk, Lansallos church, your eventual destination, can be seen on the horizon to your right.

As you round a cove, stay on the coastal path ignoring tracks off to the left.

Pass over two small boardwalks adjacent to a stile and climb away to pass out of the field through a gap in the boundary. The coastal path passes a bench and over a stile before descending to a bridge across a stream just before the isolated cove of Lansallos Beach. Cross the nearby stile and then turn left to follow a track away from the beach. Pass through two gates and continue up the shady track to reach the church once again. At the church, continue straight ahead to return to your car.

Moderate

WALK NO.

38

DISTANCE

3.5 MILES

TIME

2 HRS

MAP REF.

ORDNANCE SURVEY
LANDRANGER 201

174
518

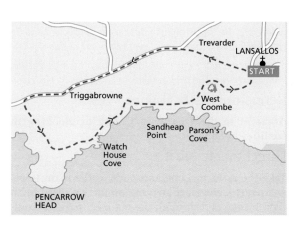

LOOE & KILMINORTH WOODS

Divided into East and West Looe by a tidal river estuary, Looe is a popular family holiday resort as well as an active fishing port. There are many opportunities for boat trips and the town is the centre for shark angling in Britain. The South East Cornwall Discovery Centre, adjacent to the main town car park at West Looe, is well worth a visit. As well as promoting green tourism in the area, the centre has a video and photographic exhibition, all of which is included in the centre's free admission policy. As an alternative to travelling to the town by car, you might like to consider the Looe Valley Regional Railway which runs between Liskeard and the town. Originally constructed to transport granite and copper ore, the line's eight miles passes through the delightful countryside of the East Looe river valley before reaching Looe close to the start of this walk.

The 3 mile circular route starts with a climb through woodland and across farmland before reaching the West Looe river. The walk returns to Looe via a lovely, riverside woodland path.

Refreshments & Toilets

Adjacent to the Discovery Centre overlooking the start point car park. Alternative facilities in Looe.

Directions to start

Take the A387 to Looe and park in the main town car park in West Looe (also signed Discovery Centre). If arriving on the Liskeard to Looe regional railway, walk across the river bridge and through the main car park in front of the Discovery Centre.

Walk Directions

Walk through the car park, away from Looe centre, towards the heavily wooded slopes of the West Looe river. Pass the information board and head up towards a gate (a sign indicates ahead a riverside walk to Watergate). Do not pass through the gate, instead bear left in front of the gate to take a path climbing steeply through woodland that is easily traced.

Ignore left and right detours to reach a path junction (striped waymark post and bench). Continue straight across and immediately bear right to reach a broad track crossing in front of you. Cross the track and take a right bearing path that continues up through the trees again in front of you. Pass through a gap in a bank and turn left to walk alongside it. This leads up to a wooden stile.

After the stile, take a diagonal path across a large arable field (i.e. following roughly in the same direction as from the start of the climb through the trees). If the field has been planted however, you may find it easier to follow the field boundary. At the top of the field, there are two gates. Pass through the one on the right and in the next field, again head for the right one of a pair of gates.

As indicated by the yellow waymark arrow, turn right after the gate and walk downhill adjacent to the right hand side. At a further gate, continue in the waymark arrow direction, bearing left away from the hedge to follow a wire fence. The field

narrows into a track where there is a gate. Bear right through a further gate and reach a metalled lane.

Turn right past Kilminorth Farm and descend sharply past a right hand bridleway signed back to Looe. At the bottom of the lane, attractive cottages are passed before reaching a public footpath sign indicating a right turn. It is now a case of following the woodland path back along the river towards Looe. At one point the path forks with the waymark arrow indicating a diversion inland. This is because the original path descends to the foreshore - which can flood at very high tide. Whichever path you take, they eventually meet to return to Looe.

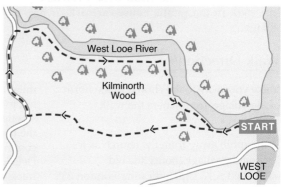

ST BREWARD ON BODMIN MOOR

Situated on the western flank of Bodmin Moor, St. Breward is over 700 feet above sea level and boasts Cornwall's highest church and inn. This ensures far reaching views for the walker with the wooded Camel valley a main feature of this short but fairly arduous circuit that starts from the church.

St. Breward's stout granite cottages were built from local stone. There are still two active quarries, the granite from which was used in many famous building projects such as Blackfriars Bridge and Singapore Harbour. Some of Cornwall's finest kaolin (china clay) is also found in the area; the pottery at Wenfordbridge to the south of St. Breward, has strong associations with Bernard Leach whose influential work is now held in a museum at St. Ives.

The geography of the area can lead to muddiness after heavy rain so ensure you have the appropriate footwear.

Refreshments & Toilets

There are a couple of shops in the village as well as the Old Inn public house.

Directions to start

From the A39 just south of Camelford, take the B3266 signed to Bodmin and St. Austell. After approx. 4 miles, turn left signed to St. Breward and then left again to enter the village from the north, close to the church. If you intend to use the facilities at the Old Inn, park in the public house car park. If not, there are various places to park in the village.

Walk Directions

Make your way to the church in the north of the village, from where the walk commences.

Walk uphill away from the church as if leaving the village (notice the old enamelled A.A. sign indicating London 235 miles away!). Shortly after the sign, turn left to take a public footpath that proceeds through gorse. Far reaching views testify to the height of the village, with Britain's first commercial windfarm, situated at Delabole, to your right. At a fork in the track, take the right hand fork, pass through a gate and head across the field to a stone stile.

Continue on a path through brambles and scrub, descending parallel with the wall on your right. At a waymark post with a yellow arrow and red rectangle, bear left to continue downhill. Pass through a small copse and continue your descent to a metal gate which is adjacent to a direction sign indicating your route to Coombe. Continue in the direction of the waymark arrow following an escarpment from where there are lovely views across the wooded Camel valley. Through a wooden gate into an area of woodland, slowly descending as you walk.

Bear left, continuing ahead on a broad farm track. Shortly after a sign for the aviaries on your left, pass between two houses and bear right on to a public footpath. Through a wooden gate and across the field to a wooden stile. Cross the second field ahead, following a waymarked track through trees. After a wall stile, pass through a wooden gate, remembering as always, to close the gate as the path here runs through animal enclosures. Through a further gate and walk ahead with ponds off to your right. A footbridge leads to a further stile and a metalled lane.

Turn left up the lane climbing steeply to a T junction next to a detached stone house. Turn left, crossing a stream before going immediate right to follow a path that leads between the old corrugated building and the stream you have just crossed.

The path climbs into woodland, crossing a tributary and meandering up between granite boulders. Follow a wire and granite post fence (far reaching views again) as it bears right to reach a stone stile. The track now continues to pass between houses and reach a residential lane via a stone stile. Turn left (public footpath sign indicates Tuckingmill) and cross a cattle grid. Just before the track drops down to a house, cross a wooden stile, turning immediate right up the side of the wire fence to cross a stone stile.

Walk uphill alongside conifers, crossing a further stone stile to walk to the left of school playing fields. At the top left hand corner, pass over a further stile and proceed straight ahead between hedges. Walk through a wooden gate and across a farm entrance to return to the main road in front of the Old Inn. From here, return to your car.

Moderate

WALK NO.

40

DISTANCE

2.5 MILES

TIME

2 HRS

MAP REF.

ORDNANCE SURVEY
LANDRANGER 200

098 774

CRACKINGTON HAVEN & THE STRANGLES

A classic Cornish walk, following an outbound route along towering coastal cliffs before returning to the start point via an attractive streamside path through a wooded valley. The walk turns inland shortly before the climb to Cornwall's highest cliff; the height already gained allows a panoramic view down the continuous series of headlands that stretch down this part of the north Cornish coastline.

Crackington Haven grew up around a small port which exported slate from nearby quarries and imported coal and timber. A grandiose plan in the 1830s to construct large breakwaters and develop 'Port Victoria' thankfully never took place and would have caused irreparable damage to the sleepy hamlet and bathing cove that you can enjoy today.

Refreshments & Toilets

Toilet block, pub, cafes and beach shop at Crackington Haven. Refreshments available in season at the National Trust Trevigue Farm (halfway around the route).

Directions to start

From the A39 between Bude and Camelford, follow signs to Crackington Haven from Wainhouse Corner. Park in a small car park adjacent to the river bridge in front of the Coombe Barton Inn.

Walk Directions

Turn left across the road bridge and then take an immediate right to follow the coast path just above the Surf Life Saving Club building. Pass through a kissing gate, past the tennis courts to a further kissing gate leading on to the coastal path. The path climbs to Bray's Point, from where there are views across Tremoutha Haven to the headland of Cambeak.

Continue towards Cambeak, passing through two kissing gates and across two boardwalks which have stiles at either end. After descending towards a third boardwalk, turn inland (left) on a narrow path up the valley (this diversion from the headland of Cambeak itself is part of a National Trust restoration project). Pass over a further boardwalk and climb steadily to reach the coastal path once again (notice the contorted rock strata on Cambeak to your right).

Turn left to follow the coastal path, gaining height steadily. In the distance, beyond the Strangles Beach, can be seen the rocky bulk of High Cliff, at 731 feet above sea level, Cornwall's highest. At a waymark post, bear left and descend to cross a stile that leads to steps, continuing ahead along the right hand boundary of a field. Pass above the Strangles Beach and descend to find a track to your left with a post signed Trevigue (right leads down to the beach).

Turn left, heading inland, to climb broad steps and follow a path between hedges to a kissing gate and parking area. Turn left along the lane and walk up to Trevigue Farm. Follow the road as it bears left in front of an initial entrance to farm buildings, reaching a gravel track that leads to the main entrance to Trevigue. Here, bear right on to the gravel track and walk to a stile on the left hand side of the farm.

Head across the field in front of you, crossing a wooden stile next to a pair of farm gates. Descend towards the tree lined valley ahead. A gap in the fence at the bottom leads to a right bearing track that descends to a path junction.

Do not cross the stile here, instead turn left along a farm track that runs along the left hand side of a stream (often wet and muddy). Continue along the valley path, ignoring diversions off the main track. After some distance, take the concrete walkway that crosses the stream right. Turn left to follow the arrow directions and cross a small stream via a concrete walkway. Follow a broad track, through a gate, leading back to the village and your car.

Moderate

WALK NO.
41

DISTANCE
3 MILES

TIME
2 HRS

MAP REF.
ORDNANCE SURVEY
LANDRANGER 190
144
968

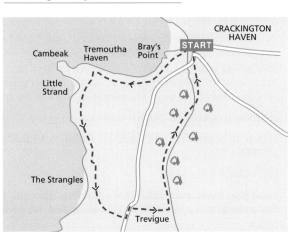

87

EFFORD BEACON & THE BUDE CANAL

A lovely five mile circular walk combining broad grassy coastal cliff paths with a return alongside Bude Canal, home to several nature reserves. Efford Beacon provides far reaching views and is reached from Bude via Compass Point, site of an unusual octagonal storm tower which has the compass point markings that have given the viewpoint its name.

After crossing fields to Helebridge, the level walk is quiet and peaceful with only the presence of an occasional rowing boat. In the last century this tranquil scene would have been filled with canal boats transporting sand and lime to the inland agricultural areas to redress acid soils. Plans at one time to link the canal with the River Tamar at Launceston, so creating passage between the Bristol and English channels, came to nothing with much of the canal abandoned in the 1880s.

Refreshments & Toilets

Toilets in start point car park, all facilities in Bude. Tea room near end of walk (01288 361015).

Directions to start

Head into Bude from the A39 via Stratton. Take the first exit on the first mini roundabout you come to and park in the Crescent car park where there is a large and interesting visitors' centre.

Walk Directions

From the car park turn left, cross over the bridge in front of the Falcon Hotel, turning right to proceed along a residential road overlooking the canal. Proceed towards the canal entrance. At the end of the cul-de-sac, climb steps and pass through a wooden kissing gate, turning right along a path that leads towards Bude's breakwater. Before reaching the breakwater, turn left at a waymark post and head up the downs to the unusual eight sided building on Compass Point. An information board gives details of the storm tower's history.

Continue on the broad grassy coastal path to Efford Beacon, passing through a large kissing gate. From here, you can, on a clear day, see Lundy Island to the north and the white radar dishes at Coombe. From the Efford Beacon viewpoint (trig point marker), follow the coastal path ahead descending and then ascending to pass through a gate. Pass through a further 2 kissing gates and run parallel with the road at Upton. Continue on past the Chough Hotel.

The path takes you past a parking area (with a confusing information board), sited on the cliff side of the road and shortly after this, the path leads you to the old Salthouse an 18th century salt store now converted to a holiday home. A sign says 'Private, please use footpath in rear of cottages'. Here, leave the coastal path, turning left to head for the road. Cross the road (Marine Drive) and follow a public footpath to Helebridge. The Bay View Inn you will notice,

is a few yards down the road away to the right.

Cross the field uphill making for the top left hand corner. Proceed straight ahead into the next field, following the obvious path. Climb over a stile and walk with the field boundary on your right. Ahead of you are the white washed cottages of Marhamchurch. Beyond a gate and stile, bear left, descending the field diagonally in the direction of Helebridge.

Cross a stile, continuing in the same direction before following the track left across a further stile next to a gate. Turn right along a concrete road before turning left across a stile shortly before a bridge. This leads across a field to a further stile that provides access to a tow path running along the left bank of the canal (signed to Bude). Continue on a level path through occasional gates to Rodd's Bridge, here, cross and return to your car via the towpath on the right of the canal.

Moderate

WALK NO.

42

DISTANCE

5 MILES

TIME

3 HRS

MAP REF.

ORDNANCE SURVEY
LANDRANGER 190

210
059

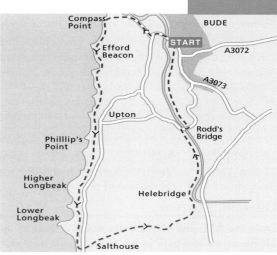

89

MORWENSTOW & HIGHER SHARPNOSE POINT

Just a short distance from the Devon border in the far northern corner of Cornwall, Morwenstow has an isolation quite unlike most other parts of Cornwall. Windswept cliffs and relatively few visitors at any time of year, make this a superb place to get away from it all and forget about the rest of the world.

Morwenstow's churchyard is full of the graves of shipwrecked sailors; the white figurehead of the wrecked 'Caledonia', appearing to almost walk between gravestones, is a particularly poignant sight even on bright sunny days. Responsibility for the figurehead lies with a previous incumbent of the church, Reverend Robert Stephen Hawker, who from 1834 until his death in 1875 saw to it that sailors wrecked on this coastline received a Christian burial. A hut built from driftwood which Hawker used to watch for wrecks, can be visited in the course of this walk and is known as one of the National Trust's smallest properties!

Refreshments & Toilets

Rectory Farm provides refreshments during the main season (01288 331251). The Bush Inn public house is at the end of the walk.

Directions to start

From the A39, just over 2 miles north of Kilkhampton (north of Bude), follow signs to Morwenstow and park in the parking area between Rectory Farm and the church.

Walk Directions

Proceed past the detailed N.T. information board and walk down the lane above the church to a kissing gate. Proceed ahead along the obvious path to the right of the field boundary in front of you. Pass through two kissing gates to reach the coast path. Pass left through a kissing gate and proceed ahead, a signed diversion down the cliffside allows you to see Hawker's Hut.

Continue through a kissing gate and follow the path, Higher Sharpnose Point is ahead on the right. The route descends adjacent to a wire fence to reach the Tidna Shute Valley. Cross the stream via a boardwalk and pass over a stile. Then follow a path that leads up to reach an old coastguard shelter. Great care should be taken if you decide to walk out on to the whaleback of a headland at Higher Sharpnose.

The coastal path passes below twisted rock strata to reach a stile that leads to a coastal path diversion away from the eroding cliffside. A short walk up a narrow valley leads to a second stile and two boardwalks. Clearer views towards the stark, white satellite dishes at Coombe are provided. Follow a broad path beside the wire fenced field.

Cross a stile and follow the edge of the field before passing over a further boardwalk to reach a path leading left between the wire fence and a hedge. Here, do not continue through the gate gap ahead (acorn sign), instead turn left and follow the path that climbs gradually away from the coast. Cross a stile to continue on a broad track, further stiles and a gate lead to a lane and a parking area. Walk ahead to find a stone stile on the left opposite the farm buildings at Stanbury.

Head across the field to a stile on the opposite side. Continue across the second field to a wooden stile next to a metal farm gate. Pass beside the historic property of Tonacombe (private) to a wooden stile. The track passes through a small copse, leaving via two stiles. Cross a small field to a stile beside a gateway, follow the right hand side of the field, descending to a stile that leads into a narrow track. This descends towards the wooded Tidna valley, crossing a wooden stile to a path junction.

Take the right fork down to cross the stream via a slate bridge. Pass a N.T. sign and over a stile, turning right up steps to reach a wooden stile. Head up the field to a further stile. Here, turn left to cross a stile and head towards the left hand side of the Bush Inn. Through a wooden gate to reach the road, turning left to return to your car.

Moderate

walk no.

43

distance

3MILES

time

2HRS

map ref.

ORDNANCE SURVEY
LANDRANGER 109

207
154

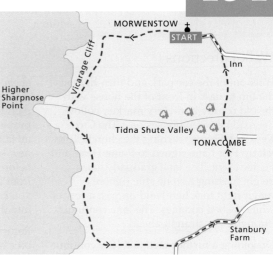

91

CAWSAND, PENLEE POINT & RAME HEAD

Rame Head is one of the great Cornish headlands, providing far reaching views across the adjacent Whitsand Bay and towards, it is said, the Lizard Peninsula some 70 miles away! The walk around Lillery's Cove towards the headland is classic coast path walking, the 12th century stone chapel on the headland at first just a mere dot on the horizon.

The walk starts from Kingsand and its neighbouring village of Cawsand. Today they are essentially one settlement although until the mid 19th century, Kingsand was in Devon with Cawsand in Cornwall. Close to the walk start, you will pass a house with the old boundary line indicated on the wall. An unusual grotto built into the cliffside at Penlee Point provides panoramic sea views before continuing on the aforementioned enjoyable ramble to Rame Head.

Refreshments & Toilets

In both Kingsand and Cawsand (i.e. at the start of the walk).

Directions to start

From the A374 to Torpoint, take the B3247 signed to Millbrook and follow signs to Kingsand. Park in a signed car park next to the Halfway House Inn. If full, use the car park at Cawsand and walk back down the road to start from St. Andrew's church.

Walk Directions

Walk out of the car park and turn right at the Inn to pass in front of the house with the old county boundary marker. Follow the road between houses past The Cross Keys Pub before reaching the church. Turn left up Pier Lane signed to Rame Head and Penlee Point. The lane gradually gains height, passing a stone stile (ignore a rough right fork here) and on past a row of whitewashed cottages. The lane continues through trees straight ahead.

On joining a further metalled lane continue ahead to pass a house on the right hand side. Shortly after the house, take the right path fork (the left goes into M.O.D. property) and climb to reach another metalled lane. Continue ahead, passing a new housing development on the right before emerging to enjoy the sea views from Penlee Point. By bearing left here, you can explore the grotto literally built into the cliffside.

Return from the grotto and proceed ahead on a broad path. In the far distance is your destination, Rame Head. The metalled lane leads to a wooden stile, after which the coastal path continues on a more typical earthen track. The coastal path climbs gradually. As you continue around Lillerys's Cove, walk past a sign for Rame Church and proceed across a stile. The footpath continues across an open field before reaching a viewing point. Follow the path in front of you towards Rame Head, ignoring diversions from the main route. Walk up to the chapel to enjoy the headland's far reaching views.

Retrace your steps from the chapel, bearing left to follow a path through gorse. At a waymark post, bear left to follow the coastline over a boardwalk bridge across a small stream. Continue around Queener Point (views are across Polhawn Cove to Whitsand Bay) passing a bench to descend on steps with the view ahead over a large white property. Continue to a wooden stile, passing through an open field and above a tennis court.

Cross a further stile and at a track fork, bear left to head down steps to reach a gravel track. Rejoin the coastal path by crossing over the gravel track as indicated by a waymark arrow and walk down some concrete steps. At the bottom of the steps follow the direction of the waymark arrow which takes you along a track parallel but below the level of the gravel track you previously crossed.

Walk past a sign which states the coast path is on the left over a stile. As the track begins to climb, ignore this stile and continue up until you rejoin the gravel track approx. three quarters of the way up. From here walk up to the main road and then proceed ahead (downhill) with Plymouth Sound in front of you.

As the road bears right, look out for two metal gates, to the left of which is a wooden stile. Cross this stile and head down to the bottom of this field, keeping to the right hand boundary. Ignore the gap on the right hand side and continue to the bottom of this field. A well worn path leads through a gap into a second field, here turn right and descend towards a gate.

Cross the adjacent stile and turn right on the road, walking up to the T junction and turning left in front of a pair of attractive cottages. Follow the road back towards Cawsand, bearing right where the road forks and walking down to the church met earlier. From here return to your car in Kingsand.

Moderate

WALK NO.
44

DISTANCE
5 MILES

TIME
3 HRS

MAP REF.
ORDNANCE SURVEY
LANDRANGER 201
434
505

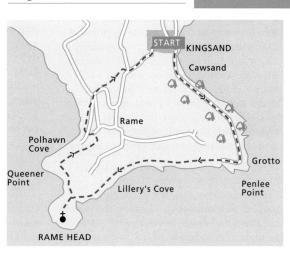

MOUNT EDGCUMBE & CAWSAND BAY

One of the longer walks in this book and certainly one of the best. Located on the far eastern edge of Cornwall overlooking Plymouth, this area can easily be missed by visitors to the county which is a shame as there is much to recommend it. Mount Edgcumbe Country Park, from where this walk commences, has 800 acres open free to the public with 5 historic formal gardens and a wild deer herd. The historic house itself is a faithful reconstruction of the original 16th century building which was destroyed by a stray incendiary bomb in 1941. The house is open during the main holiday season, the admission charge providing an opportunity to view the Edgcumbe family paintings, furniture and effects.

From the country park, this walk follows the coast path along the Minadew Brakes to the old smuggling village of Kingsand. Turning inland, the walk gains height on the climb to Maker Church, allowing broad views across Plymouth Sound where you will spot pleasure craft and warships alike.

Refreshments & Toilets

Toilets just above Cremyll ferry and in Kingsand. Refreshments at Mount Edgcumbe Country Park.

Directions to start

From the A374 to Torpoint, take the B3247 signed to Millbrook and Mount Edgcumbe Country Park. After Millbrook follow signs to Mount Edgcumbe Formal Gardens before turning left into the car park at Cremyll (approx. 2.75 miles from Millbrook).

Walk Directions

Emerge from the car park and cross the road, turning left to walk along the pavement towards the sea. Bear right to walk up to the gates of Mount Edgcumbe. After the gates, turn left signed to Formal Gardens and Orangery Restaurant. The splendour of Mount Edgcumbe House can be seen to your right. Pass through the large archway and around the right hand side of the restaurant, attractive gardens with a fountain are to your right. Continue between tall hedges before joining a path that provides views across Plymouth Sound towards Devil's Point. In front of an old battery fortification, detour left up steps to enjoy the view, along with the cannons pointing towards Drake's Island.

Returning to the path, leave the gardens through a gate and proceed along a concrete path bearing left at the fork marked 'amphitheatre'. Keeping the pond and classical temple to your right, pass through trees to reach a gate (to your right

are the impressive remains of a tower). Continue to a path fork, taking the upper path through bracken before resuming a coast path just above the shoreline. Plymouth Breakwater, guarding The Sound, can be seen through the trees to your left.

At a waymark post next to a path fork (and a small brick construction), keep left to descend along the shoreline for a short distance before climbing through woodland once again. Follow the waymark posts, turning sharp right in front of a wooden fence. Follow the track as it turns left to go through a gate. At a broad track, turn left and pass underneath a stone arch. Continue on a broad woodland path from where the piers of Picklecombe Point can be seen through the trees below left.

Pass a small stone built grotto before reaching a track junction. Bear left to take the lower path and go through an old metal gate to a wooden gate. From just after the gate, the twin settlements of Kingsand and Cawsand can be seen ahead. Cross a stile and turn right on a metalled lane. After about 40 yards, cross a stile next to a gate on your left. An obvious path now leads ahead to Kingsand. (Where the path splits, take either as they soon rejoin). A number of seats provide a tremendous vantage point across Cawsand Bay. On nearing Kingsand, walk past an information sign and pass through a gate.

At the main road, bear left then immediate right to walk along Lower Row (the Rising Sun pub is below left). Walk ahead past cottages to a junction, here continue on passing the Maker Community Hall. Turn right up a metalled lane (Earl's Drive). This climbs steeply away past allotments and behind an overgrown old fort.

Proceed to pass in front of farm buildings before turning right at a road junction signed to Fort Picklecombe. Head downhill for about 80 yards before turning left over a stile signed to Maker Church. Cross the field in line with the telegraph poles, over a further stile and field before taking a third stile and crossing a concrete track. Take the path to the left of a large white property and cross a stile. Walk ahead to a wooden stile, after which turn sharp right and head to a stile in the top of the field (views to Torpoint and Plymouth Sound). Bear right to visit the churchyard.

Turn right out of the churchyard

and walk ahead signed to Empacombe. Pass through a gate, crossing the main road to follow a track downhill through the woods. On reaching a broad track, cross half right and continue on a fairly well defined path through the trees. Zig zag downhill to reach a wooden stile. Walk across a meadow diagonally to reach a track that runs to a gate. Cross the road and over a stile to follow a public footpath to Empacombe around the bottom of fields.

At Empacombe Harbour, follow instruction signs to pass around the inlet. On the other side, turn right through a gap in the wall and leave via a metal gate. Walk up the tarmac driveway for a few yards before bearing left along a grass track. Continue the walk on the path that follows the shoreline back to Cremyll, enroute passing a metal gate and three wooden stiles. At Cremyll, turn right up the main road to return back to your car.

Moderate

WALK NO.

45

DISTANCE

6 MILES

TIME

4 HRS

MAP REF.

ORDNANCE SURVEY
LANDRANGER 201

454
534

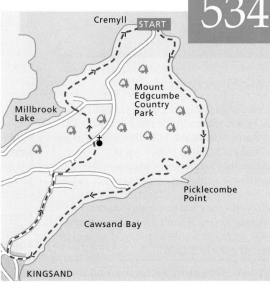

95

ROSEMULLION HEAD &
THE CARWINION VALLEY

From the sheltered and popular bathing spot of Maenporth Beach near Falmouth, this walk follows the coastal path around Rosemullion Head to the edge of the broad Helford River. Large parts of the coastal path here pass across land in the care of the National Trust, Rosemullion Head an example as well as a believed site of an Iron Age Cliff Castle. After turning inland to walk up the splendid Carwinion Valley, the remainder of this circular route is via meadows and open countryside.

Refreshments & Toilets

Both are available at Maenporth Beach.

Directions to start

From the A39 Penryn bypass, turn off at the Hillhead roundabout near Falmouth signed to Constantine then Maenporth. Follow the narrow country road to park just behind the beach. (If this is full, there is a larger cafe car park on the opposite side of the road).

Walk Directions

From the parking area sited virtually on the beach, return to the road and turn left. At the bottom of the hill, turn left on to the coastal path. Initial views are of Falmouth's Pendennis Castle and the lighthouse at St Anthony Head. Continue on the coastal path as it skirts gardens before opening out to provide views towards Rosemullion Head. Climb some steps and skirt a stile to proceed along the bottom edge of a field.

Descend steps, cross a stile, descend more

steps to pass Bream Cove before entering into the National Trust property of Nan Sidwell. After going through the wooden gate leading to Gatamala Cove, take the left fork at an acorn post. Proceed over three further stiles to a gate with a stone stile at Rosemullion Head.

Keeping to the left, round the headland, follow the path at the edge of the field across a stone stile and through a meadow. Cross a small wooden bridge and a couple of stiles with views south to the Lizard

Peninsula. Pass through the area of light woodland at the NT property of Mawnan Glebe, ascending wooden steps adjacent to an acorn sign and over a stone stile and kissing gate. Walk about 150 yards before bearing left over a stone stile and continuing on the coast path. Shortly pass over another stone stile and a little further on down some steps.

Pass through two kissing gates to a small area of pebbly beach, following the path around the back of an old hut to a larger pebbly beach (a boathouse and slipway is here). On the other side of the boathouse is a wooden gate with a sign on it directing you to Maenporth up the Carwinion Valley plus a further sign to Mawnan Smith. Follow the woodland path through two kissing gates until you cross over a small stream via a slate bridge.

At this point take the right hand path, still continuing on the woodland walk through a wooden gate until you ascend on to a track and over a stile attached to a wooden gate. The track emerges past some houses to a lane leading to a main road. Turn left towards Mawnan Smith village and after a couple of hundred yards, turn right on a public footpath signed to Meudon (the sign is directly opposite Mawnan Bowling Club). Cross a stone stile and follow the edge of the field.

Over a further stone stile adjacent to a metal gate on the far side of the field and keeping the hedge to your right, pass over another stile and head for the farmyard

gate. Do not go through the last farmyard gate, instead turn left keeping to the edge of the field, passing over a stile to descend in a narrow field. Once this becomes a track, pass through a broken gate on the right and walk diagonally left across the meadow toward a stone gap in the hedge negotiate this field clockwise keeping to the edge.

Do not cross the stream, but follow the bottom edge of the field, passing through wooden posts into an area of woodland. Take the right hand fork for about 50 yards before bearing left at a post with a green arrow. Continue through the woods descend steps, turn right into a clearing at the bottom of a meadow. Follow the yellow arrow. Go past a granite post and along the bottom of a second meadow. Keep following the yellow waymarks, over a stile and down into Maenporth.

Moderate

WALK NO.
46

DISTANCE
5 MILES

TIME
3 HRS

MAP REF.
ORDNANCE SURVEY
LANDRANGER 204
790 297

CHAPEL PORTH & ST. AGNES BEACON

From the scenic National Trust cove of Chapel Porth, itself a onetime mining location, this walk passes the splendidly preserved mine engine house at Towanroath, one of Cornwall's most photographed mining remains. Built to house a pumping engine for the nearby Wheal Coates Mine, it is a reminder that this walk is through an area that was once one of the great bastions of Cornish mining. The walk concludes from the 629 feet high summit of St. Agnes Beacon, on a clear day, one of Cornwall's most far reaching viewpoints.

Refreshments & Toilets

The National Trust provide toilets and refreshments during the season at the car park in Chapel Porth.

Directions to start

Follow the B3277 St. Agnes road to the outskirts of the village. Turn left to follow the brown National Trust signs for Chapel Porth. Follow signs along a narrow road and park in the small N. T. car park at the bottom of the hill adjacent to the beach.

Walk Directions

Turn right from the car park to start back up the entry road before taking a sharp left onto the coastal path. The climb above the beach approaches a small valley, bear left to follow the coastal path and in turn reach the mine stack at Towanroath. Continue above steep drops to the sea, a coastguard practice post can be seen away to the right. Shortly after a crevice in the cliffside (perhaps an old mining adit?), the path bears right to climb fairly steeply for a short distance.

Turn left onto the broad track at the top, heading towards a bench. Pass the bench and continue straight ahead, ignoring the waymarked fork left which returns to the coastal path.

Proceed onto a metalled road, bearing around to the right, leaving the coast behind. As the road starts to bear around to the left towards the coastguard lookout, turn right following an obvious path through the heather. Proceed ahead in the direction of St. Agnes Beacon to reach a clearing, crossed by telegraph poles. Here, bear left, emerging on to the metalled road once again. Turn right and ascend to the main road.

Cross the road and take the right hand path to the top of St. Agnes Beacon. Follow the path over the Beacon summit, descending to continue on the right hand path where the track divides adjacent to a rocky outcrop. The path descends and starts to bear right before turning left and passing a mine shaft warning post.

Continue through the gorse before turning right onto a broad track which leads to the road. Turn right, passing a farm, before eventually turning left into the Wheal Coates National Trust car park. From the bottom of the parking area, proceed onto a broad track for 15 yards before bearing left towards Chapel Porth. The track eventually becomes broader before veering left to pass a bench, descending into the valley and heading back to the car park.

Moderate

WALK NO.
47

DISTANCE
3.5 MILES

TIME
2 HRS

MAP REF.
ORDNANCE SURVEY
LANDRANGER 203
698
496

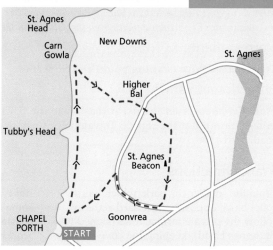

ST. AGNES & THE JERICHO VALLEY

St. Agnes was once a hub of the mining industry in Cornwall, an industry that employed thousands of men, women and children and once boasted two thirds of the world's copper and tin output. This walk explores a landscape steeped in mining history, starting from the delightful beach and surfers' haven of Trevaunance Cove, near St. Agnes. A coastal path ramble turns inland to St. Agnes, passing the 'Stippy-Stappy' miners' cottages before descending back to the coast via a streamside path through the picturesque Jericho Valley. A preserved water wheel is passed before a coast path return to Trevaunance Cove. Inland views from the path reveal the many mine building remains in the area.

Refreshments & Toilets

Trevaunance Cove (starting point) and St. Agnes.

Directions to start

From Perranporth on the north coast, take the B3285 to St. Agnes. As you approach the village, turn off at the sign to Trevaunance Cove. A car park is situated at the end of the road, above the cove.

Walk Directions

From the smaller car park, which has a toilet block opposite, turn hard right to follow the private tarmac road (signed to St. Agnes Head), keeping the cove on your right. Pass through a gate to climb up some steps to the top of the cliff. The coastal path passes capped mine shafts, workings and one or two conveniently placed seats. Views offshore are to Bawden Rocks, also known as Man and his man.

Approximately half a mile from the top of the previously mentioned steps, the path eventually rises to a path junction. Immediately in front and above you is a large and fairly modern farm residence. At the path junction just before the sign "NT Newdowns Head" take the left path (if you pass a wooden bench situated below a farm wire fence, you have gone too far). The path climbs between gorse hedges with the large farm building off to the right (Bawden Manor Farm). Turn left onto a metalled lane for approx. 200 yards before turning right to follow a broad track which starts next to two telegraph poles after passing Doble Foods on the right.

The track passes the occasional house before eventually bearing left in front of farm buildings to reach a main road. Cross and head up Beacon Road on the opposite side. Continue up a slight hill to pass between cottages. Shortly afterwards, cross a stone stile on the left indicating a public footpath to village. Descend adjacent to a stone wall, passing over a stone stile in the right hand hedge at the bottom.

Cross the field diagonally via the obvious path, crossing a stone stile in the opposite bank. Cross the next field through an opening in the wall, descending via the next field/stile to follow a track that leads into the village. Cross the road at the bottom of the track and descend via a narrow lane to turn left into the main street of the village. Continue around past the church, following the road signed towards Perranporth, passing the 'Stippy-Stappy' miners' cottages.

Follow the main road out of the village passing two pubs. Continue ahead over the brow of the hill to reach the sign for the hamlet of Barkla Shop. Immediately after this is a left turn which should be taken, following a steep lane downhill. At the bottom, turn right crossing a footbridge over the stream to follow a streamside path through light woodland past Jericho Cottage. Continue down the valley.

At the main road, turn left, crossing a bridge before bearing right on the hairpin bend across a stile and onto the coastal path. A fairly steep climb is rewarded at the top with panoramic views. Follow the coast path above Trevaunance Cove, eventually descending to the Driftwood Spars Hotel. Turn right and return to the car.

Moderate

WALK NO.
48

DISTANCE
4.5 MILES

TIME
2.5 HRS

MAP REF.
ORDNANCE SURVEY
LANDRANGER 203
721
515

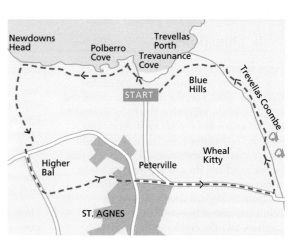

ST. MAWES & ST. JUST-IN-ROSELAND CHURCH

Nestling within the shelter of the Carrick Roads estuary, St. Mawes is a boating mecca and popular destination for many visitors to the Roseland Peninsula. The resort's 16th century castle is generally regarded as the most attractive of those built by Henry VIII and is only a short walk from the busy harbour and shops. Perhaps even more famous is St. Just-in-Roseland Church, its creekside location and lush subtropical gardens affording one of the most attractive settings of any church in the country.

From St. Mawes, this circular walk passes along the peaceful Percuil Creek before turning inland to climb towards St. Just-in-Roseland Church. The walk to and from the church is via National Trust fields that afford panoramic views across the Carrick Roads to Falmouth, one of the world's largest natural harbours.

Refreshments & Toilets

All facilities in St. Mawes including toilets in car park (start point) and next to Church in St. Just.

Directions to start

From the A39 Truro to St. Austell road, take the A3078 and follow signs to St. Mawes. Park in the main St. Mawes car park. (Alternatively, use the King Harry Car Ferry signed from the A39 at Playing Place between Truro and Falmouth. St. Mawes is reached from St. Just-in-Roseland via the A3078).

Walk Directions

From the car park, turn left to take the main road away from the village centre. Continue ahead on the pavement above the small beaches, following the road around to the left into a residential area. At a right turn to Freshwater Lane, turn sharp right down a tarmac lane towards the creek. Just before reaching the creekside, turn left to climb a few steps indicating a public footpath to Percuil Creek. This path continues ahead between the bottom of gardens and the creek before eventually reaching a metalled lane.

Turn right to the boatyard before crossing a slipway left to resume the creekside path. Cross a wooden stile adjacent to a bungalow, bearing right around the bottom of the field until reaching a house on the right (about half way along the field), screened by a tall hedge so that only the roof is visible.

Here, turn left noting the yellow waymark post in front of the tree. Proceed uphill, heading towards an opening in the hedge. Within a few yards the path divides. Ignoring the public footpath sign to Porthcuel Creek, continue to the brow of the hill and then through a small wooden gate adjacent to a wooden field gate.

Continue on the track through the middle of the field, passing over a stile by a metal gate to a second field keeping the hedge to your immediate right. A good view of Percuil Creek can be seen down to the left and through a gap in the hills the English Channel can be observed, indicating how narrow the peninsula is here. Directly ahead can be seen Falmouth Bay.

In the bottom right hand corner of the field, pass through a gap in the hedge and a metal gate to emerge in a cul-de-sac. Bear left and right to follow a further left out of the estate to the main road. Turn right and proceed uphill for half a mile past the fire station to the large water tower on the horizon, next to a garage.

Shortly after the water tower, turn left, then immediately right crossing a stile to enter the National Trust property of Tregear Vean. The path now proceeds ahead adjacent to the hedge and parallel to the road across a series of stiles, the vast expanse of the Carrick Roads estuary is displayed before you.

At the final stile, turn left down a track indicated as a public footpath to St. Just. Descend crossing two stiles before crossing over a driveway and descendng to St. Just-in-Roseland church. Pass through the lychgate into the churchyard. After exploring the church and its lush memorial gardens, follow the path left along the creek, passing through a swing gate and some trees before reaching a boatyard.

After the boatyard, turn right on a metalled lane indicating a two mile public footpath to St. Mawes. Bear around to the left in the driveway, passing Bar Point House and turning left shortly before a bungalow and pass through a gate and into a field.

Follow waymark arrow to right and through wooden gate into fields offering views to Falmouth and Pendennis Castle. From here, it is a straightforward track back towards St. Mawes crossing stiles and meadows enroute. Eventually, the path crosses a stile to leave the NT property of Newton Cliffs behind and proceeds on a road in front of some large houses. Continue ahead towards St. Mawes Castle and follow the main road downhill back into St. Mawes.

Moderate

WALK NO.

49

DISTANCE

5.5 MILES

TIME

3 HRS

MAP REF.

ORDNANCE SURVEY
LANDRANGER 204

848
333

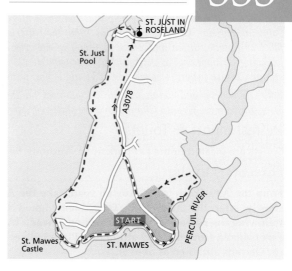

ST. ANTHONY HEAD & LIGHTHOUSE

Situated at the very tip of the Roseland Peninsula, St. Anthony Head has been fortified in one form or another since the Napoleonic Wars. Along with the neighbouring castles at Pendennis and St. Mawes, the St. Anthony Battery helped defend the strategic Carrick Roads estuary and approach to Falmouth harbour. Until as recently as 1956, the battery was fully operational with its magazine filled with ammunition and ready to fire. The site was acquired by the National Trust in 1959 following a reappraisal of the country's defensive needs. St. Anthony Lighthouse, one of 12 in or around Cornish waters, was built in 1834 and is now automated and controlled from the Lizard.

Both the battery and lighthouse are encountered on this walk which includes coastal walking alongside both the English Channel and the sheltered Carrick Roads.

Refreshments & Toilets

Toilets are located in the car park at St. Anthony Battery (start point).

Directions to start

From the A39 Truro to St. Austell road, take the A3078 signed to St. Mawes. Turn off shortly after the hamlet of Trewithian signed to Gerrans. Pass through Gerrans, following the narrow lane to St. Anthony Head. (Alternatively, use the King Harry Car Ferry signed from the A39 at Playing Place between Truro and Falmouth. Follow signs for Gerrans and then as above).

Walk Directions

From the end of the car park, walk past the right turn to the lighthouse and join a narrow path passing above the toilet block. The path passes around the previous site of the gun emplacement before following a route through gorse and blackthorn bushes and maintaining the coastal path around Zone Point.

A gate and two stiles are passed before entering the National Trust property of Porthbeor. On reaching the main access point to Porthbeor Beach on your right, turn left heading across the field to a stile in the hedge next to a National Trust sign.

Turn right onto the road before taking the first left to Bohortha. Pass through the hamlet and follow the unmade lane ahead (past a postbox) indicating a public footpath to the Church of St Anthony. The track passes two gates on the right before reaching a path junction at the bottom of the track between two hedges. Take the left path signed to the church. Descend, keeping the field boundary hedge to your immediate right. At the bottom right hand corner of the field, pass over a stone stile in the hedge and descend some steps to a road. Cross the road and opposite stile to reach St Anthony church (look out for the medieval stone coffin).

Pass to the left of the church, climbing steps before bearing right to follow the coast path track uphill. At the top bear right and follow the country lane downhill. At the bottom, follow the lane around to the left to skirt the end of the creek. As you round the creek, take the stile on your left indicating a coastal path to St Anthony Head. Ascend the field, crossing a stile at the brow of the hill before descending to turn left on the coastal path. St Mawes and Pendennis Castles are now in view.

A path with stiles now continues along the coastline towards St Anthony Head Lighthouse, passing around attractive sandy coves and inlets. Cross a wooden footbridge, turning right and through a large white gate shortly before the lighthouse's old paraffin store. A tarmac track leads to the lighthouse, or turn left up steps to your car.

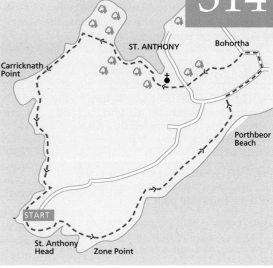

Moderate

WALK NO.
50

DISTANCE
3 MILES

TIME
2 HRS

MAP REF.
ORDNANCE SURVEY
LANDRANGER 204
847
314

105

LERRYN, ST. WINNOW CHURCH & ETHY WOODS

The tidal creek where the River Lerryn joins the River Fowey, is little known and consequently rarely busy. The lush creekside woodlands are a delight in all seasons, a network of paths date from when Lerryn was an active river port and when stream fed mills ground corn higher in the valley.

The five mile circular route follows woodland paths down the creek to the Fowey River estuary at St. Winnow Point. From here, it is an enjoyable ramble to the riverside St. Winnow church, surely one of Cornwall's most tranquil places of worship. The walk is completed via waymarked paths across open farm and park land, passing in turn the ruins of St. Winnow Mill and the Georgian manor house of Ethy.

Refreshments & Toilets

Both are available at Lerryn (start point).

Directions to start

From the eastern side of Lostwithiel on the A390 St. Austell to Liskeard road, follow signs to Lerryn. On reaching the village, cross the narrow road bridge and follow the road right to the main car park.

Walk Directions

WHEN THE TIDE IS FULL : Return by the road to cross the narrow road bridge used earlier and take the first left down a narrow lane that bears left to assume a creekside path.

WHEN THE TIDE IS LOW : Cross the stepping stones in the river and turn left onto the creekside path.

The creekside path passes in front of cottages and to the right of a house before continuing through a gate that leads into the National Trust Ethy Woods. The path turns inland for a short distance to pass alongside a small inlet, near the head of which, the path forks. Take the left fork, beside the waymark sign and cross the stream via a boardwalk to resume passage on the opposite side back towards the creek.

The woodland path continues above Lerryn Creek, bearing left onto a wide gravel track (waymark post with yellow arrow and blue circle). After a short while, leave the wide track to walk on a woodland path once again, the waymark post indicates the position left. A further small inlet is skirted (Mendy Pill) before continuing on the creekside path until you come to a few wooden steps next to a waymark post, once again bear left on the broad gravel track. This time, follow the track for its duration; the very gradual right turn leads away from St. Winnow Point in the direction of St. Winnow itself.

The broad track narrows to become an altogether smaller, shadier woodland path which gradually descends to reach a stile. Cross the stile and bear left along the bottom of the field to pass over a second stile and continue ahead in the same direction. Cross a further wooden stile and follow the path along the foreshore before turning right at a waymark post up a lane and taking a further right to visit St. Winnow church.

Pass through the churchyard, leaving via a gate at the top in front of a house. Head up the metalled road before taking the public footpath signed right, shortly before the St. Winnow Barton Farm Museum. Pass through a metal gate and follow a broad track uphill through a further gate. At the top, cross a stile next to a metal gate and head across the field diagonally towards the gate in the top right corner.

Cross two adjacent stiles and follow the left field boundary to reach a stile next to a metal gate. Bear right towards a gate and stile, afterwards walking diagonally half left towards a wooded area. Cross two adjacent stiles and follow a track adjacent the hedge and a wire fence. A stile leads left at the end, heading downhill to a further stile in the right hand boundary. Cross and turn right down a gravel lane, bearing left where the track divides (waymark arrow).

Pass the ruins of St. Winnow's Mill following a track away from the mill to reach a path junction. Here, bear left and climb through the woodland. Cross a stile at the top and walk diagonally ahead across the middle of the field, passing a large oak tree to reach a gateway.

Pass through and descend through a further gate, following the boundary bank. Continue heading to the left of a further large tree in the direction of bungalows on the right hand side. Cross the gate and proceed left through the cul-de-sac. Turn right down the lane and return to your car either by the stepping stones or by turning left in front of a cottage and returning via the road bridge.

Moderate

WALK NO.

51

DISTANCE

5 MILES

TIME

3 HRS

MAP REF.

ORDNANCE SURVEY
LANDRANGER 200

140 571

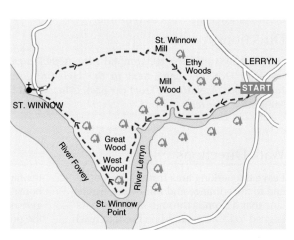

CIRCULAR WALK AROUND LOE POOL

Loe Pool is Cornwall's largest freshwater lake, formed by the creation of Loe Bar, a sand and shingle bank that dammed the once navigable River Cober. Loe Pool came into the ownership of the National Trust as part of the Penrose estate, given in 1974 and at 1554 acres the largest single land donation in Cornwall. As a consequence, the Trust have installed two small boardwalks at wetter parts of the shoreline, so facilitating a level five mile walk circuit close to the water's edge.

The Loe offers the walker a calm serenity, no doubt attractive also to the large number of birds, particularly overwintering wildfowl, that can be seen here. The sheer contrast between the waters of the lake and the sea, divided only by a sandy bank, is one of the visual highlights of west Cornwall.

Refreshments & Toilets

Neither are encountered within the course of the walk. Nearby Helston can provide both before or after the walk as required.

Directions to start

On the A3083 south of Helston, take the A394 Penzance road before turning immediately left into Degibna Lane next to the Helston Cottage Hospital, sited adjacent to the roundabout. A National Trust car park is located at the end of the lane, opposite Degibna Methodist Church.

Walk Directions

Leave the parking area from the opposite end to the entrance and follow a concrete lane that descends through a kissing gate (signed to Degibna and Loe Pool) to reach the farm buildings at Degibna. At the house, fork left to pass through a kissing gate next to a farm gate. Follow the lane to the pool, turning right to start an anticlockwise circuit around the lake. At first glance, the size of the lake seems quite small though this is because all of Carminowe Creek and the southern end of the lake is out of view from this point.

On reaching the end of the lake, follow the path to the right of Loe Marsh, passing over a stone stile next to a gate. Walk along a path through light woodland to pass over a wooden stile, through a field and over a further wooden stile. Turn left onto a concrete lane shortly before the entrance to farm buildings.

Just before the remains of a small engine house, turn left through a gate with a National Trust sign. Cross a wooden footbridge over the River Cober, the source of Loe Pool. Continue ahead to pass through a wooden gate before turning left along a broad track through the woodland of Oak Grove. A bird hide is soon passed on the left.

Continue through the gate in front of Helston Lodge, following the now metalled lane as it leads right towards Penrose House. Follow the lane across the parkland towards the stables, bearing left in front of them to resume the circuit. The track assumes woodland again as it passes through Bar Walk Plantation. In time, Carminowe Creek comes into view on the left with the sea visible across Loe Bar through the trees ahead.

Follow the track above Loe Bar to Bar Lodge, passing through a gate next to which is an emergency telephone (an indication of the danger of swimming here). Turn left and cross the beach, heading

for the white cross on the opposite headland.

After visiting the memorial, return to the sandy path that leads alongside Carminowe Creek. A boardwalk passes around the head of the creek bearing left before leading to a track past the National Trust property of Lower Pentire. Follow a track, turning left shortly before the surface becomes metalled. This route passes through a gate to run around the edge of a field.

At the end of the field next to a bench, follow the field edge away from the water, passing through a gate to once again use a woodland track (through Degibna Wood). Where the path divides, use either as they soon rejoin. Shortly after Degibna Wood, you are back where you started the circuit. Turn right, returning to your car by the route used earlier.

Moderate

WALK NO.

52

DISTANCE

5 MILES

TIME

3 HRS

MAP REF.

ORDNANCE SURVEY
LANDRANGER 203

654
252

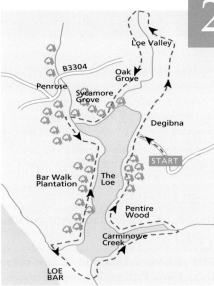

CHURCH COVE & HALZEPHRON CLIFF

Positioned to the leeward side of a small headland called Castle Mound, the church of St. Winwalloe (Gunwalloe) is on a site that has been a place of worship for over 1,000 years. The unusual beachside location of the church is made all the more interesting by the church's detached bell tower, dug into the surrounding cliffside. Dollar Cove, just to the north of Castle Mound, has been so called since the 16th century wrecking of a Portuguese treasure ship.

This figure of eight circuit reaches Church Cove from Poldhu Cove, both delightful bathing spots popular with families. The coastal path circuits Dollar Cove to Halzephron Cliff before returning via a path through the golf course back to Poldhu Cove.

Refreshments & Toilets

Both available at Poldhu Cove (start point) and Church Cove during the season.

Directions to start

From the A3083 Helston to Lizard road, turn off right after RNAS Culdrose, signed to Cury and Poldhu Cove. Park in the car park behind Poldhu Cove beach.

110

Walk Directions

Leave the car park turning right onto the road which crosses the stream via a bridge. Proceed to the bend in the road before bearing left to follow the metalled lane above Poldhu Cove. The lane leads to a small parking area at the National Trust property of Carrag-a-Pilez. A track descends from the parking area to Church Cove and provides outstanding views. Cross the back of the beach, over a wooden bridge and head towards the church.

After exploring the church at your leisure, take the broad track at the far end of the church towards the refreshments and toilet block. Here, take some stone steps to walk on the coastal path which climbs gradually to the right away from the church round Halzephron Cliff. The stretch of beach that can be seen in the distance is Loe Bar and the start of Porthleven Sands.

Follow the coastal path. Shortly after a National Trust sign for Halzephron Cliff, cross to a small parking area and turn right onto the road. At the main road, keep right and descend back to Church Cove. After passing the toilet block once again, take the metalled road bearing left.

Shortly before the end of the road, take a track left to cross a small stone bridge and enter the golf course. After a while, the path divides. Continue straight ahead climbing steadily before reaching the Mullion Golf Clubhouse and onto the main road. Turn right on the road to follow the edge of the golf course before descending back to Poldhu Cove.

Moderate

WALK NO.

53

DISTANCE
IN MILES

3

TIME
IN HOURS

1.5

MAP REF.
ORDNANCE SURVEY
LANDRANGER 203

667
200

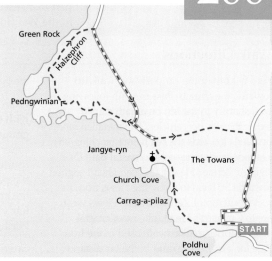

Green Rock
Halzephron Cliff
Pedngwinian
Jangye-ryn
Church Cove
The Towans
Carrag-a-pilaz
START
Poldhu Cove

The far western toe of Cornwall has long acted as a magnet for visitors to the county, the natural and symbolic attraction of Land's End by far its most popular destination. Less well known but in many ways a more striking feature, is the granite coastal landscape of north Penwith. Zennor lies at the heart of this landscape, situated in an isolated and at times harsh coastal plain, sandwiched between inland granite moors and towering sea cliffs. Small fields enclosed with irregular granite borders dominate the landscape, having changed little since their establishment over 2,000 years ago.

From the famous church at Zennor with its mermaid legend, this walk follows the striking coastal scenery from Zennor Head to Wicca Pool and onto River Cove. Turning inland up a lush, sheltered valley, the route returns to Zennor via a well used path across open countryside and farmland.

Refreshments & Toilets

Toilet block (seasonal opening), Public house adjacent to the church and the Old Chapel Cafe all in Zennor.

Directions to start

Zennor is on the B3306 between St. Ives and St. Just-in-Penwith. A parking area is provided close to the Wayside Museum.

Walk Directions

Turn left out of the car park and walk up towards the church. Pass the pub following its wall sharply to the left on a path signed footpath only, no vehicles. The metalled lane proceeds towards the sea before reaching an unmade track to reach the coastal path (N.T. sign for Zennor Head). Proceed ahead (signed towards St. Ives) to enjoy the views from the rocky outcrop of Zennor Head. Views west are to Gurnard's Head (like most coastal promontories in Cornwall, used in the Iron Age for a cliff castle) and in the far distance

the lighthouse at Pendeen Watch.

From Zennor Head follow the coastal path with the sea to your left to reach a further granite outcrop from where there are superb views towards Mussel Point, our future destination. After a steady climb, the path reaches a waymark post. Follow the arrow direction (left) and proceed on a fairly level path that starts to pass around Porthzennor Cove.

Cross a narrow stream and pass an old

waymark post before bearing left to proceed along a rocky hillside. Cross a second small stream (in dry periods, this is small enough to have dried up). The path descends to run closer to the sea. Just as it looks as if the path will actually continue to the rocks below, it turns inland to climb through a series of large granite boulders, between which at times there are only the narrowest of gaps. A short climb to a granite outcrop reveals Wicca Pool, a cove in which you will often see seals.

Bearing right, the path passes up the side of the Wicca Pool cove before climbing up the right hand side of a stream. At a waymarked wooden stile, cross left and head down granite steps to cross the stream. The coastal path climbs above Wicca Pool, passing between huge granite boulders before heading on an obvious path towards Mussel Point. Pass over a granite stile and ignoring a cairn of stones on your right continue on a grassy path to pass through a gap in the stone wall ahead. Continue, descending to run closer to the sea, offshore are rocks called The Carracks. An obvious track climbs through two stock gates and steadily away from the sea to where the path forks, just before River Cove.

Take the right fork, up the valley (leaving the coast path behind). After a streamside copse, pass wild fuschia bushes that are a blaze of colour if you are completing the walk in mid to late summer. The valley path continues before reaching a concrete driveway and metal

cattle grid. Turn right and climb past stone cottages on the right to reach a house on the left. From here, follow the vehicular track left, climbing inland for some distance. The track reaches a group of farm buildings in front of a turning area.

Turn right to walk down past Boscubben Farm, and, parallel with the sea, continue to reach Wicca Farm. Head through the farmyard, passing just to the right of the farmhouse. As the sign has helpfully indicated earlier, it is now a case of following the path in the direction of the telegraph poles back to Zennor. The route passes houses at Tregerthen before following the line of the poles across church path stiles to pass just above Tremedda Farm. From here the telegraph poles bear right away from the main road. Do not follow them, instead continue in the direction in which you have been walking over church path stiles until the tower of Zennor church acts as a guide back to the hamlet.

Tough

WALK NO.
54

DISTANCE
4.5 MILES

TIME
3 HRS

MAP REF.
ORDNANCE SURVEY
LANDRANGER 203
455
384

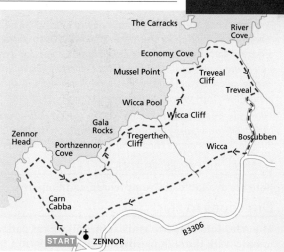

POLPERRO & CHAPEL CLIFF

Polperro is one of the more familiar names to visitors of Cornwall. Its attraction is that it remains a classic example of a Cornish fishing village. Narrow streets of whitewashed cottages lead to a well preserved harbour which can be sealed in times of rough weather. Originally developed as a fishing and smuggling centre in the 13th century, Polperro's heyday was in the 17th and 18th centuries when the fishing and processing of pilchards employed most of the village. Nowadays, some fishing remains though boat trips provide a more regular source of income.

This walk leaves Polperro to follow the coastal path along the National Trust Chapel and Raphael Cliffs. The undulating nature of the terrain makes this one of the harder walks in East Cornwall though there are ample choices for refreshments when you get back to Polperro.

Refreshments & Toilets

Both are available at Crumplehorn and Polperro.

Directions to start

The A387 into Polperro ends at the village car park at Crumplehorn from where it is a 10 minute walk through narrow streets to Polperro's famous fishing harbour.

114

Walk Directions

From the car park, walk past Crumplehorn Mill with its restored watermill on your left and head down to reach Polperro harbour. Make your way to the Blue Peter Inn on the harbour's west side (right as you look towards the sea), and climb the steps to the rear of the building, waymarked "To the Cliff".

Follow the coast path, passing a National Trust sign for Chapel Cliff. Shortly after this sign, the path forks. Keep to the lower path and continue on the undulating route ignoring other detours from the main coastal path.

At the other end of Chapel Cliff cross over a very small stream. Immediately after this, notice a commemorative plaque placed in the rock face. Keep walking until you come to about 160 steps which have to be climbed. Shortly after this you will see the National Trust sign for Raphael Cliff. Cross a wooden boardwalk over a stream. Continue on the coast path, down a number of steps, across another wooden bridge where the ascent alternates between paths and steps.

Keep walking and eventually you will descend more steps to reach a very large pointed stone pillar (Landmark). About 200 yards past this pillar but NOT as far as the wooden bridge or a sign marked "Lansallos", you will see wooden steps in the hedge on your right. Go over this stile and climb up a grass field, keeping to the right along a reasonably well defined path. Staying close to the wire fence, an old barn will come

into view on the horizon. Continue on, past a small wall and through a wooden gate. A yellow arrow sign guides you on a gradual incline, past a fingerpost. You will pass to the right of the derelict barn and through the right hand gate. From this point, on a clear day, it is possible to see as far as the Lizard Peninsula.

From here a yellow arrow directs you along a country lane flanked by high hedges. From this lane, views inland are towards Bodmin Moor.

At the end of the lane you will come to a gate that leads to a metalled road where you must turn right. The quiet country lane takes you past Raphael Farm, Landaviddy Manor Hotel and down into Polperro. Walk through the village and return to your car at Crumplehorn car park.

(If the undulating cliffs here have tired you out, you may want to take advantage of the horse cart and 'trambus' rides that run in the main holiday season between Polperro and the car park).

Tough

WALK NO.

55

DISTANCE

4.5 MILES

TIME

3 HRS

MAP REF.
ORDNANCE SURVEY
LANDRANGER 201

205
515

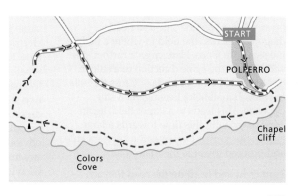

115

TINTAGEL & THE ROCKY VALLEY

Tintagel is inextricably linked with the legend of King Arthur, something that no modern visitor to the village can miss. The dramatic headland that is believed to have housed Camelot was certainly the site of a third century monastery as well as a medieval stronghold. Also dating from this latter period is the National Trust owned Old Post Office, a splendid example of a medieval manor house, restored in the fashion of the post office it was for 50 years.

North of Tintagel is the lush wooded river valley of St. Nectan's Glen, the stream from which passes through the idyllic Rocky Valley to reach the sea at Bossiney Haven. All of the above are encountered in this walk as well as St. Piran's Well and Chapel, dedicated to the sixth century patron saint of Cornwall.

Refreshments & Toilets

Toilets in car park (start point). Refreshments throughout Tintagel. Refreshments also available in season at Trevillet Mill on the approach to Rocky Valley. Further toilets and refreshments also available close to the end of the walk at Tintagel Castle (English Heritage).

Directions to start

From the A39 near Camelford, follow signs to Tintagel. Park in the car park in the centre of the village opposite the Old Post Office (N.T.).

Walk Directions

Turn left out of the car park in front of the Old Post Office, heading away from the coast to pass King Arthur's Great Halls. Follow the main road through Tintagel to pass Trenale Lane on your right and reach a public footpath sign indicating a right turn across open fields. Cross the stile and head diagonally across the field to where a hedge meets a wire fence. Here cross a further stile and head in the same direction to a stile in the opposite hedge boundary. Cross the stile to enter a small field, leaving via a stile opposite. This leads to a larger field, again cross diagonally, this time towards a large gate in the corner. Pass over the adjacent stile and proceed towards the main road.

Turn right and head up the road to reach

some houses. Turn left between the houses and go through the gate of Barn Cottage to cross a stile at the rear of the property. Keep the hedge on your left until you come to a corner where it goes off to the left down the field. Bear right across the field to some stone steps just to the right of a metal gate near two electricity pylons. On reaching a metalled lane, turn left and walk for 150 yards to where the road bears off to the left. A public footpath sign indicates passage right across two stiles before crossing the field and descending to a kissing gate that leads into woodland. Descend bearing right on the obvious track to reach a bridge over the stream, a large signpost indicates St. Nectan's Glen leading off to the right.

Here, bear left following the sign to St. Piran's Well and Trethevey. Ascend from the woodland onto a metalled lane and continue until reaching St. Piran's Well and Chapel. Turn left in front of the Well and then left onto the main road, taking care as there is no roadside path and it can be busy. Descend into the valley and as you pass a parking area on the left, fork right to follow the path past Trevillet Mill and Millers Restaurant towards Rocky Valley. Cross the stream via the footbridge and continue to a series of ruined buildings. In on the right hand side are some early Bronze Age (e.g. 4,000 years old) rock carvings in the form of intricate maze like patterns.

The path crosses a wooden bridge to follow the left bank of the stream down to the sea. After this wooden bridge you will shortly come to a waymark post which indicates the start of the coastal path. Just below and to the right of this post is a wooden bridge leading on to the northern coastal path. Do not go in this direction but turn left on to the southerly coast path to reach another waymark post.

A diversion here allows you to watch the sea surging up the narrow gorge. Note also how the action of a mini waterfall in the stream has smoothed and carved the rock. From the waymark sign the coast path climbs steeply out of the valley to enjoy views across to the headland of Willapark. The path descends steps to cross the access path to Bossiney Cliffs (NT). Climb the opposite steps and cross the stile before descending to a wooden footbridge where there is a National Trust sign for Willapark.

The coastal path climbs steeply before emerging onto a grassy plateau. Keep to the seaward path taking an optional diversion to Willapark Headland itself through the first gap in a wall on the right. Return and continue heading right through another gap in the wall to follow the coastline back towards Tintagel.

Pass through a wooden kissing gate in the wall, the dramatic, tall cliffs of Willapark are on your right. The path leads to a small gap in the wall followed by a wooden gate and then to the National Trust Barras Nose sign, Barras Nose being the first property to be acquired by the National Trust in Cornwall. Ignore a path to your left and descend to cross the stream in front of Tintagel Head (entrance fee required to access the English Heritage maintained castle).

Turn left past the exhibition shop and toilets and head up the wide path back to Tintagel. This is fairly steep and if you are really tired, you can pay to be taken to the top in a Landrover. On reaching Tintagel, continue ahead to return to your car.

Tough

WALK NO.

56

DISTANCE

4MILES

TIME

3HRS

MAP REF.

ORDNANCE SURVEY
LANDRANGER 200

056
885

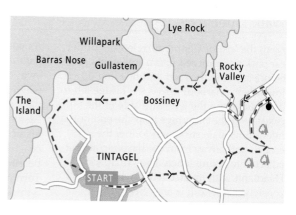

Boscastle's harbour area is wonderfully scenic, its notoriously jagged entrance a challenge as much for today's boatmen as in its heyday when it was a busy port and one of the few safe havens for boats on this part of the coast. N.B. This walk was walked before the dramatic floods in August 2004, but Boscastle remains one of the most attractive harbours in Cornwall.

From the harbour, this walk follows the coastal path to the Willapark Headland, site of an Iron Age cliff castle. The distinctive white coastguard lookout is, of course, a more modern addition. From here the route follows a path above dramatic cliffs before turning inland and returning to Boscastle via open farmland. This latter area is referred to on the O.S. map as Paradise, a perfect description of the far reaching views along this part of the coastline.

Refreshments & Toilets

Toilets in the start point car park. Refreshments from shops, pubs and tea rooms in Boscastle village and at the harbour (toilets here also).

Directions to start

Follow signs to Boscastle from the A39 Bude to Camelford road. Park in the large car park in the centre of the village where there is a North Cornwall Visitor Centre.

Walk Directions

From the Visitor Centre, turn left out of the car park and proceed past a row of shops before crossing the road and heading down towards the harbour. Cross the bridge left to continue down the left hand side of the river. After the moorings near the end of the inlet, climb slate steps and follow the coastal path away from the harbour, at first adjacent to a wire fence. The Willapark Headland with its distinctive white coastguard lookout is above right.

As you round a deep chasm, the coastal path divides. Instead of continuing inland, away from the sea as indicated by the waymark post, bear right to enjoy the views from Willapark (there is a bench beside the old coastguard building). After visiting the Willapark headland, rejoin coastal path by descending on a right bearing path back to a gap in a slate wall. Turn right and walk to a path junction with a yellow arrowed waymark post.

Here bear right and continue ahead reaching steps which descend to a wooden stile. Cross and meander ahead to a further stile. The coastal path climbs ahead before descending steps that leads to a further stile.

Climb away by way of the coastal path and follow the well worn path across the field ahead. Pass over a slate wall and walk past an acorn post to a waymark post (marked Trevalga). Here, leave the coastal path (which bears right), and pass through a kissing gate to continue ahead on a farm track to reach a metalled lane. The lane climbs ahead before bearing left through the hamlet of Trevalga and on to reach a main road.

Cross the road and walk up a steep hill opposite. Pass the slate built converted chapel and continue to climb before reaching a track bearing left (public footpath sign). Turn left in front of the Old Rectory driveway entrance columns to take a track marked with a waymark post (can be overgrown) leading to a gate. A waymark post indicates the way ahead along the right hand edge of the field, from where, stunning views along the coastline commence. When the field hedge turns right go straight on to the gate.

Continuing in the same direction, pass through the farmyard at Trehane, observing waymark posts until you reach a field edge. Continue ahead (or turn right and walk alongside the field boundary if crops are growing in the field). Follow the direction of the waymark arrows which take

you through a gap in the field boundary.

From here, bear half left across the field in the direction of the church. On reaching the opposite boundary, do not pass through a gate gap but follow the waymark post and walk just to the left of the field boundary. Cross a stone stile in the corner and walk directly ahead across the field to pass over a wooden stile (about half way down the field). Continue to a slate stile next to a waymark post and reach a semi metalled lane.

Turn left and follow the lane down to the main road. Cross to reach the pavement and turn right, walking towards Boscastle. The road eventually bears left (signed New Road) and descends (unfortunately without a pavement). Shortly after passing Forrabury Hill on your left, turn right to take a pedestrian access to Boscastle. Turn left into Old Road and proceed downhill back to the start point.

Tough

WALK NO
57

DISTANCE
3.5 MILES

TIME
2 HRS

MAP REF
ORDNANCE SURVEY
LANDRANGER 190
101
914

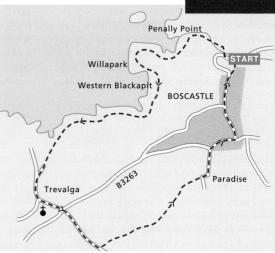

BOSCASTLE, ST. JULIOT'S CHURCH & VALENCY

This is a fairly arduous walk though the walker is rewarded with terrific views of Boscastle's picturesque harbour and the Pentargon inlet where there is a small waterfall. From the coastal path, the route heads inland to reach St. Juliot's church. It was here that a young Thomas Hardy met his future wife Emma Gifford. Hardy's original profession was that of an architect, arriving in 1870 to supervise the restoration of the church before marrying Emma four years later. Like St. Juliot's church, the Valency Valley is much the same today as when the Hardys walked here, a lush woodland valley with a streamside path that leads back to the harbour.

The North Cornwall Visitor Centre found in the car park is well worth a visit and has a series of displays about the area in which you will be walking (free admission).

Refreshments & Toilets

Toilets in the start point car park. Refreshments from shops, pubs and tea-rooms in Boscastle village and at the harbour (toilets here also).

Directions to start

Follow signs to Boscastle from the A39 Bude to Camelford road. Park in the centre of the village next to the North Cornwall Visitor Centre.

Walk Directions

From the Visitor Centre, turn left out of the car park and proceed past a row of shops before crossing the road and heading down towards the harbour. Shortly after passing a bridge that crosses the stream, notice the Harbour Light gift shop, a one storey building with an amazing crooked roof. Here, bear right up a tarmac lane following the direction of the coastal path waymark post. Pass in front of a row of cottages from where there are excellent vistas over the harbour area.

As you pass above the harbour walls, follow the coastal path signed right to climb slate steps that lead up the hillside. The path climbs steadily (a fish shaped weathervane is to the left). Follow the coastal path which runs alongside a slate wall until reaching a waymark post adjacent to a stile (depending on the rainfall in the previous weeks, the white gash of Pentargon waterfall can be seen at

the head of the inlet on this part of the walk). Cross the stile right and keep left to a further wooden stile. Resume the coastal path around Pentargon before descending down steep wooden steps to cross a footbridge over the stream that fuels the waterfall. Climb away from the valley following the path around Beeny Cliff to Seals Hole before ascending steeply to reach steps with a waymark post indicated as Fire Beacon.

After resting at a memorial seat, cross over a stile keeping to the left edge of the field. After a further stile, follow the obvious coastal path through 2 fields. Come up over a stile with 3 arrows indicating coastal path straight on, do not cross this stile. Follow 3rd arrow right with field boundary to your left. The track begins in this field corner. Take the track that leads away from the coastline between two overgrown hedges. On reaching a metalled road, turn left and pass a house on the left before turning right at a road junction. Immediately after two houses and some farm buildings, go down a rough track leading off to the left indicated by a public footpath sign (do not follow a public footpath sign before these houses).

Cross the stile adjacent to the gate and head downhill close to the right hand side. Look ahead on the opposite side of the valley to the right of the farm buildings to see a stile which will be encountered shortly. Continue downhill to reach a fairly well hidden and sometimes slippery boardwalk across a stream. Cross the stile and emerge to climb up to negotiate the stile spotted a few minutes ago. Enter the field (used by visitors during the summer) and proceed diagonally to the far right top hand corner where there is a further stile. Assume the farmtrack and continue on to reach the main road. Cross the road to steps signed as a public footpath.

Cross half left to a stile, continuing across the second field to an opposite stile. Enter a third field, heading half right to a stone stile that leads to a fourth field. Cross diagonally right towards a metal gate. Pass through the adjacent kissing gate and keep left in a fifth field to reach a wooden farm gate. After the gate, turn left to reach a road. Turn right and follow the road to St. Juliot's church which is usually open for you to explore.

Leave via the stile at the bottom of the churchyard before crossing

right over a stile to follow the left hand side of the field. Cross another stile continuing in the same direction to reach a further stile on your left. Cross and turn diagonally half right to pass through a gate gap where there is a series of public footpath signs. Follow the direction for Newmill, passing through a kissing gate to enter woodland. The woodland path continues for some distance before passing through a gate and onto a gravel track to climb away from a white house via the driveway.

Bear left shortly after the gate to follow the broad track on the left. Do not bear off towards buildings, continue straight ahead on a track that leads to a kissing gate. Pass in front of a white property and assume the woodland path that runs above the River Valency. Pass the footbridge that leads left to Minster church. Now enjoy the walk back to Boscastle, passing through occasional kissing gates as you follow the river towards the village

Tough

WALK NO.
58

DISTANCE
6 MILES

TIME
3.5 HRS

MAP REF.
ORDNANCE SURVEY
LANDRANGER 190
101
914

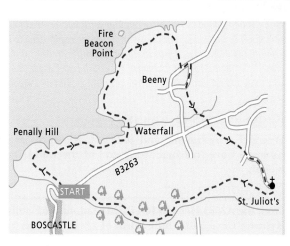

Fire Beacon Point

Beeny

Penally Hill

Waterfall

B3263

START

St. Juliot's

BOSCASTLE

KYNANCE COVE, GEW-GRAZE & PIGEON OGO

Kynance Cove is rightly known as one of the most beautiful parts of Cornwall and has been a popular destination for visitors since Victorian times. Multicoloured serpentine rocks, turquoise seas and golden sands at low tide make the cove popular with bathers and families, whilst the rich flora and fauna of the surrounding landscape and the many areas to explore make it a favourite with naturalists and walkers. From the National Trust parking area, the route strikes inland before turning to reach the coast at Gew-graze. It is then a case of following the coastal path back to Kynance, the height of the plateau on which you walk is best illustrated by the plunging cliffs at Pigeon Ogo, passed near the start of the coastal section.

Refreshments & Toilets

Seasonal refreshments and toilets at Kynance car park (start point). Seasonal cafe at Kynance Cove (reached at the end of the walk). Year round facilities in nearby Lizard village.

Directions to start

From the A3083 Helston to Lizard road, turn off following brown National Trust signs to Kynance Cove half a mile north of Lizard village. The car park is reached via a toll road

Walk Directions

Walk to the flag pole next to the information hut in the furthest of the two parking areas. Do not go through the gap towards the cove, instead turn right and head up to the gap in the wall at the corner of the field. Turn left onto a gravel track. As you descend to a dip, note initial views towards Asparagus Island and Kynance Cove itself.

Ascend on the gravel track to reach a boulder marking the start of a grassy track leading off to the right. Follow the track until reaching a wide worn track crossing left to right in front of you. Turn right for approximately 25 yards before bearing left on a narrow path which descends to a slightly boggy area with stepping stones across a stream. Pass through a gate to reach a sign indicating you have entered the English Nature Reserve of Kynance Farm.

The path leads away ascending to the left before reaching a small waymark post with a green arrow indicating permissive bridelway, follow a series of similar clearly marked arrows through the gorse until the path arrives at a junction of 3 gates in the corner of a field. Turn right following the arrows.

A broad track between hedges leads past a ruined farm building and through a gate heading towards Kynance Farm. Just in front of the farmhouse take a left turn to follow a track down the valley and a tiny stream winding its way to the sea. The path eventually crosses the stream to head up cliffs on the left hand side of the valley (if you are not in any hurry, explore the cove below with its miniature waterfall).

As the path ascends, note the gloriously different shades of rock that make up the cliffs here. The route is now dictated by the coastline with the path bearing around chasms and small headlands, the most notable of which is Pigeon Ogo, a dramatic incursion by the sea below 200 foot cliffs. As you near Kynance, the outline of Lizard Lighthouse can be seen on the horizon. A yellow waymark post marks the descent to the cove where refreshments can be obtained in the season.

At lower states of the tide, cross the beach in front of the cafe to follow the path back to the car park. Otherwise, follow the gravel track to the left of the cafe as it zig zags away from the cove. On reaching a broad track crossing from the left, turn left to reach the grassy path used earlier in the walk. By turning right on this path you will reach the two boulders from where you can return to your car.

Tough

WALK NO

59

DISTANCE

3.5 MILES

TIME

2 HRS

MAP REF.

ORDNANCE SURVEY
LANDRANGER 203

688
133

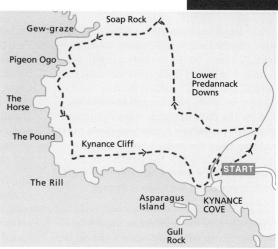

LAMORNA COVE & TATER-DU LIGHTHOUSE

The evocative Lamorna Cove, in the far west of Cornwall, is the starting point for a lovely walk with much to see. The brilliant whiteness of the Tater-du Lighthouse provides a striking contrast to the green and blue hues of the land and seascapes. Weathered granite rocks are passed on the way to the secluded St. Loy's Cove, from where a peaceful woodland path commences the second half of the walk.

A megalithic chambered tomb dating from 5,000 years ago is encountered shortly before the Merry Maidens, Cornwall's most famous stone circle. The 19 stones are said to be of maidens turned to stone as a punishment for dancing on a Sunday. The Pipers, a pair of 14' stone pillars in a neighbouring field are said to have been musicians who suffered the same fate as the dancers.

Refreshments & Toilets

Refreshments and toilets available at Lamorna Cove. Lamorna Wink pub in the valley above the cove and Tea Garden enroute (seasonal) at St Loy.

Directions to start

Take the A30 to Penzance. Follow signs for Newlyn before proceeding on the B3315 to follow signs for Lamorna. Park behind the harbour.

Walk Directions

Leave the cove, walking past the cafe towards the coastline (heading west). A metalled lane leaves the harbour below left to follow a gravel track onto the coast path. A path through a tumbled granite landscape leads past a small stone cross. Follow the path up steep steps until you come to two yellow arrow waymark posts. On rounding the rocky knoll at the top, initial views towards the lighthouse at Tater-du can be seen. From here the coastal path is smoother with fewer granite intrusions.

Shortly before the lighthouse, pass over a wooden fence stile with stone steps on the other side and onto a wooden/stone stile. Pass the gate and driveway down to the lighthouse continuing ahead on a now broad track that leads to a large metal gate. Cross the adjacent stile and follow the track towards cottages (distant views ahead are towards Logan Rock). Near the end of the cottages, turn off the driveway to resume the left bearing coastal path indicated by a waymark post.

The coastal path here is quiet and fairly overgrown in places though clearly traceable. The path descends before crossing a wooden stile next to a stream boardwalk. Pass through a small copse

using a boardwalk before proceeding on the coastal path to the granite outcrop of Boscawen Point. From here there are excellent views across St. Loy's Cove, our next destination. From Boscawen Point, the path turns inland a little before passing over a wooden stile and descending towards the cove. Stepping stones provide passage over some of the damper areas.

As you approach the cove, a grassy path leads into a wooded area. Large rounded boulders provide the route for just a few yards across St. Loy's Cove, take great care as this is ankle twisting country! At the back of the beach follow a track that leads in front of a large metal gate. At the end of the wall, turn right and follow the direction of a yellow arrowed waymark post. This climbs through a wooded valley with a stream, passing a stone stile and some steps to reach a wooden stile. Turn right after the stile and follow the path to a further waymark post next to a clump of trees. Take this right turn and cross the stream to follow the obvious woodland path, eventually emerging from the woodland to reach a metalled road on right.

Turn left to follow the road, initially uphill. A lichen covered stone cross is passed shortly before granite driveway columns.

Follow the road for 1 mile before joing B3315 for a short distance, go right reaching Tregiffian Barrow, an English Nature sign provides information on the megalithic chambered tomb

which was constructed some 5,000 years ago. From the barrow, follow the grassy verge to a stone stile next to a metal gate. Enter the field and proceed to the Merry Maidens stone circle. A path leads from the middle of the circle to the corner of the field diagonally opposite the stone stile. Cross over the stile to walk across the field passing a telegraph pole and heading for the line of 3 further telegraph poles. Note two further large standing stones in a field to the left, these are The Pipers referred to as part of the Merry Maidens legend.

Pass over a stile adjacent to the main road, bearing right down a metalled lane signed to Menwinnian Country House Residence for the Elderly. Pass a converted chapel and the entrance to Menwinnian Country House. A lane indicated as a public bridleway descends to cross a track before reaching the road. Turn right and descend through the delightfully wooded valley, passing the Lamorna Wink pub on the way back to the cove and your car.

WALK NO.

DISTANCE

5 MILES

TIME

4 HRS

MAP REF.

ORDNANCE SURVEY
LANDRANGER 203

450
241

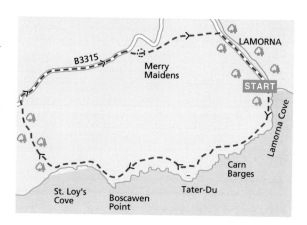

Your walks record

Use these pages to record the date on which you complete
each walk and any notes you may have.

1	
2	
3	
4	
5	
6	
7	
8	
9	
10	
11	
12	
13	
14	
15	
16	
17	
18	
19	
20	
21	
22	
23	
24	
25	
26	
27	
28	
29	
30	

31	
32	
33	
34	
35	
36	
37	
38	
39	
40	
41	
42	
43	
44	
45	
46	
47	
48	
49	
50	
51	
52	
53	
54	
55	
56	
57	
58	
59	
60	

index